THE LAST OF US™

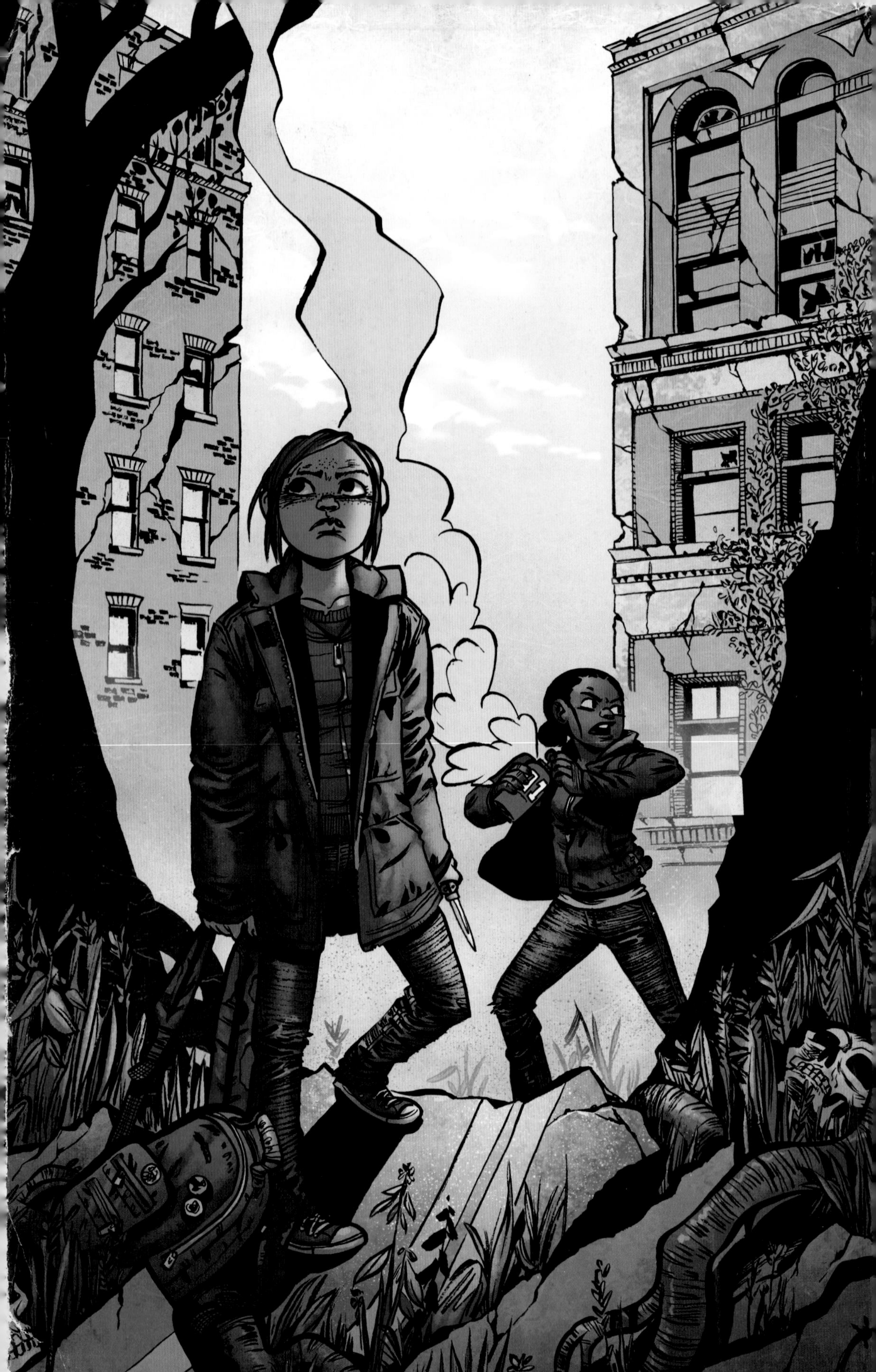

Illustration by **FAITH ERIN HICKS** with **CHRISTINA STRAIN**

THE LAST OF US™

AMERICAN DREAMS

WRITTEN BY
NEIL DRUCKMANN
AND **FAITH ERIN HICKS**

ART BY
FAITH ERIN HICKS

COLORS BY
RACHELLE ROSENBERG

LETTERS BY
CLEM ROBINS

COVER AND
CHAPTER BREAK ART BY
JULIÁN TOTINO TEDESCO

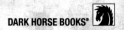

DARK HORSE BOOKS®

President and Publisher **MIKE RICHARDSON**

Editor **BRENDAN WRIGHT**

Assistant Editor **IAN TUCKER**

Original Series Editors **BRENDAN WRIGHT** and **RACHEL EDIDIN**

Original Series Assistant Editors **IAN TUCKER** and **JEMIAH JEFFERSON**

Designer **TINA ALESSI**

Digital Production **ALLYSON HALLER**

Special thanks to **NICK McWHORTER** at Dark Horse and **ERIC MONACELLI** and **ARNE MEYER** at Naughty Dog.

THE LAST OF US™: AMERICAN DREAMS

This volume collects issues #1–#4 of the Dark Horse comic book series *The Last of Us: American Dreams*.

Published by
Dark Horse Books
A division of
Dark Horse Comics, Inc.
10956 SE Main Street
Milwaukie, OR 97222

DarkHorse.com
TheLastOfUs.com

Library of Congress Cataloging-in-Publication Data

Druckmann, Neil.
The Last of Us : American Dreams / written by Neil Druckmann and Faith Erin Hicks ; art by Faith Erin Hicks ; colors by Rachelle Rosenberg ; letters by Clem Robins ; cover and chapter break art by Julian Totino Tedesco. -- First edition.
     pages cm
ISBN 978-1-61655-212-1
1. Graphic novels. I. Hicks, Faith Erin. II. Rosenberg, Rachelle. III. Tedesco, Julian Totino. IV. Robins, Clem, 1955- V. Title.
PN6727.D79L37 2013
741.5'973--dc23

                          2013026271

First edition: October 2013
10 9 8 7 6 5 4 3 2 1
Printed in China

CHAPTER ONE

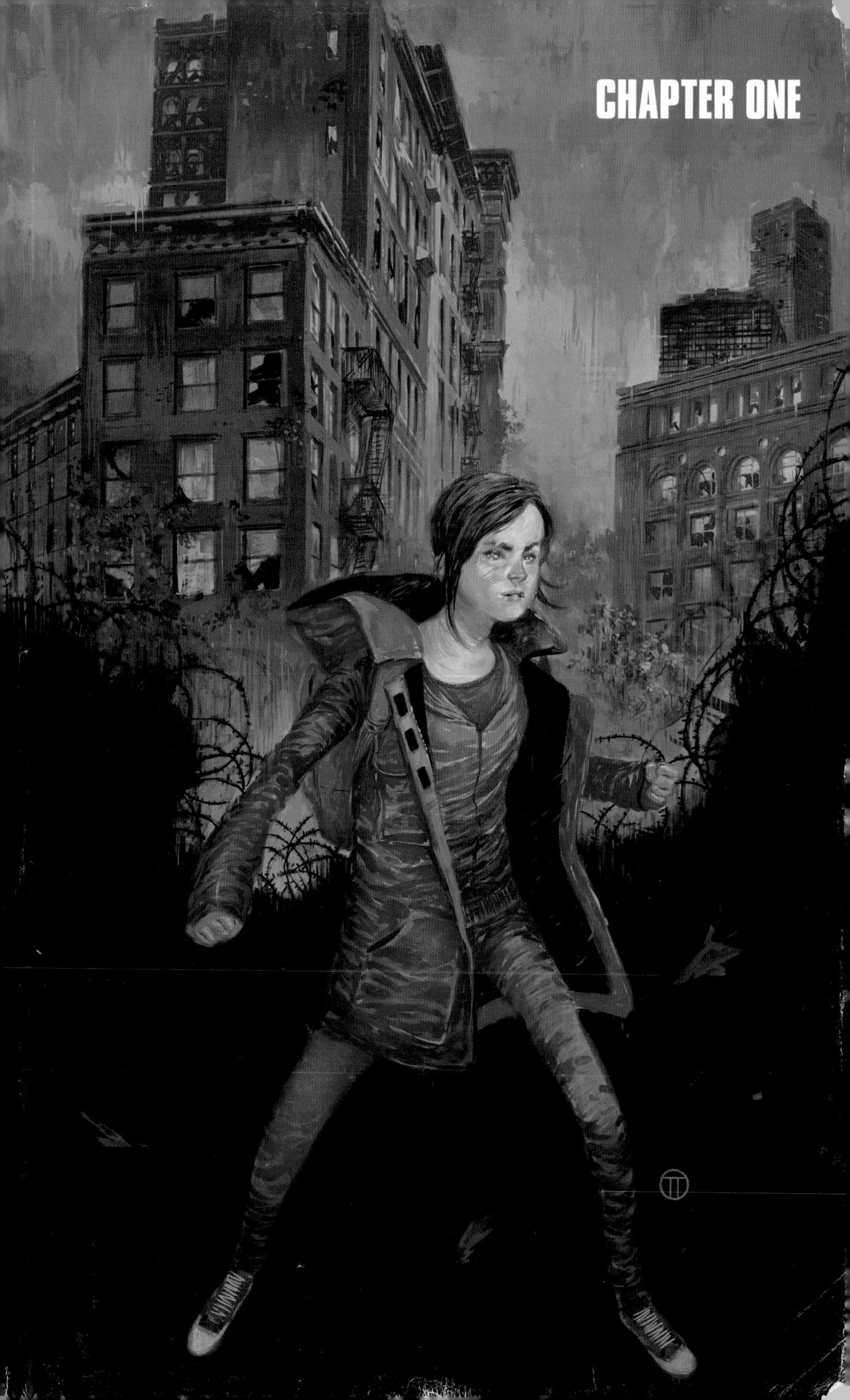

This story takes place before the events of the game *The Last of Us*.

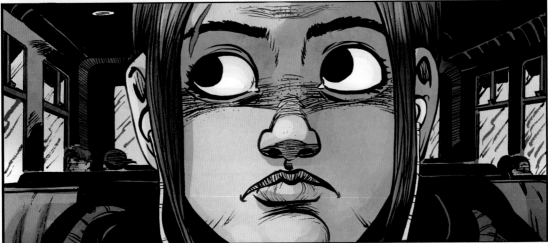

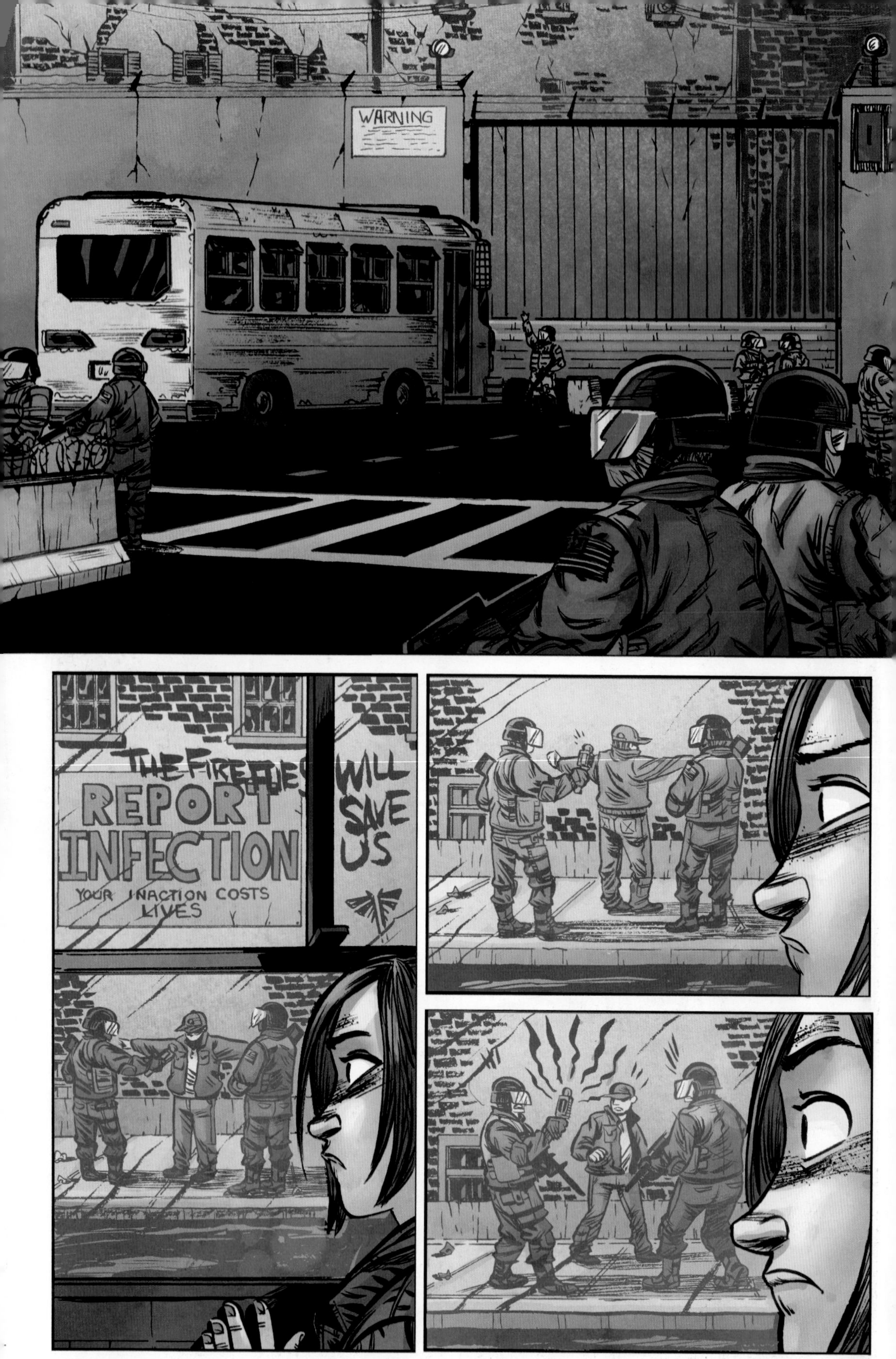
WARNING
THE FIREFLIES WILL SAVE US
REPORT INFECTION
YOUR INACTION COSTS LIVES

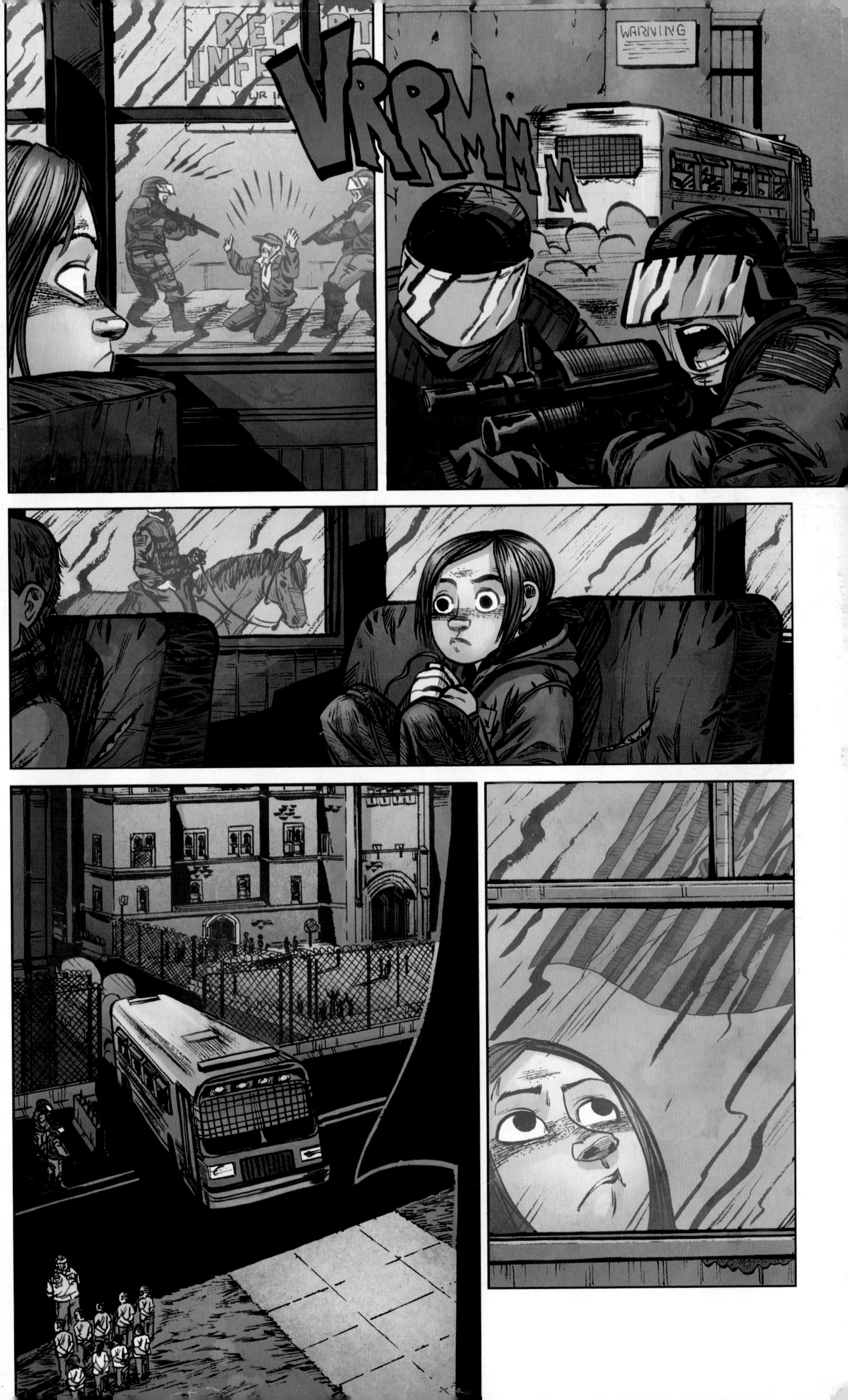
WARNING
VRRMMM

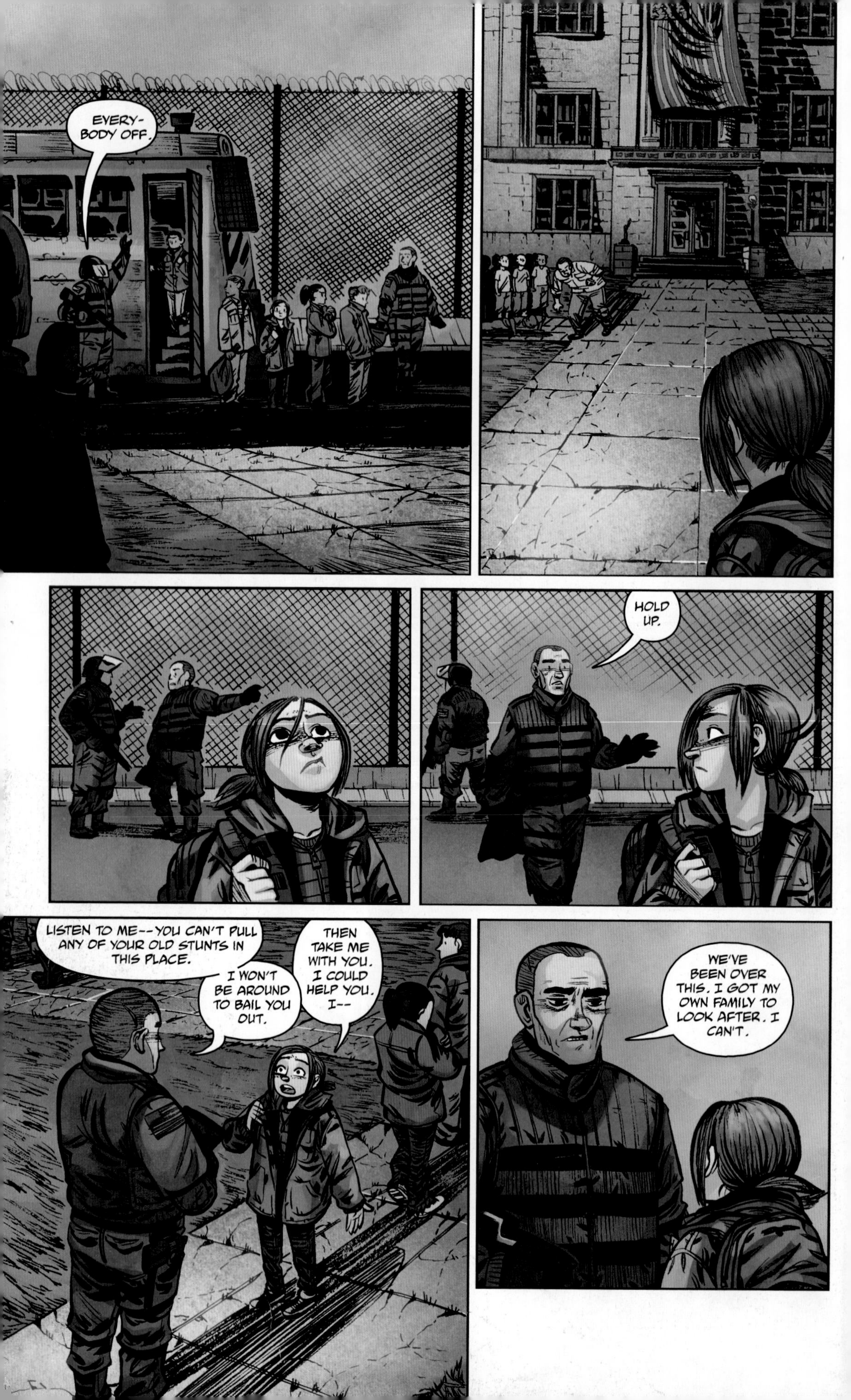
EVERY-BODY OFF.
HOLD UP.
LISTEN TO ME--YOU CAN'T PULL ANY OF YOUR OLD STUNTS IN THIS PLACE.
I WON'T BE AROUND TO BAIL YOU OUT.
THEN TAKE ME WITH YOU. I COULD HELP YOU. I--
WE'VE BEEN OVER THIS. I GOT MY OWN FAMILY TO LOOK AFTER. I CAN'T.

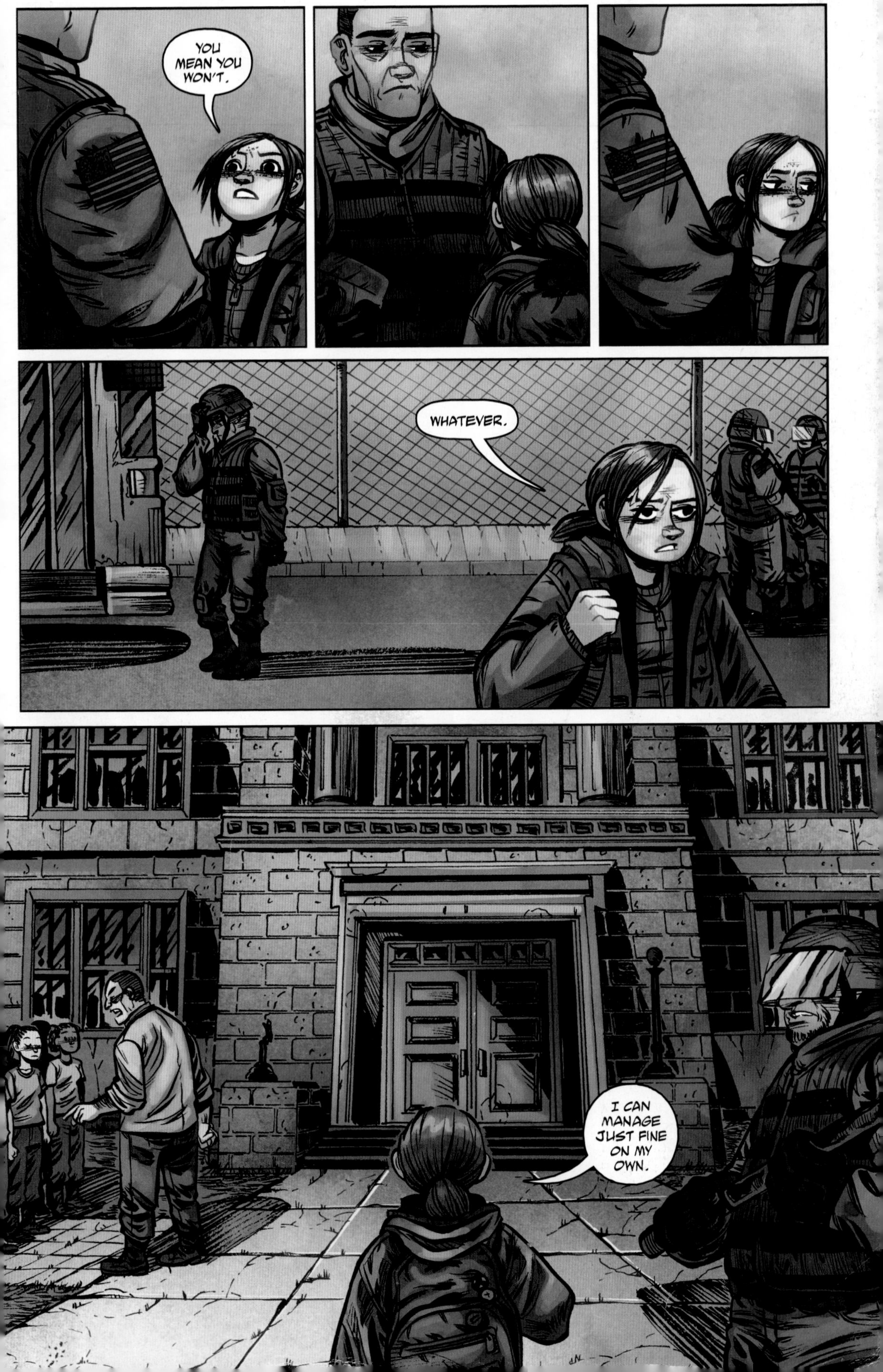
YOU MEAN YOU WON'T.
WHATEVER.
I CAN MANAGE JUST FINE ON MY OWN.

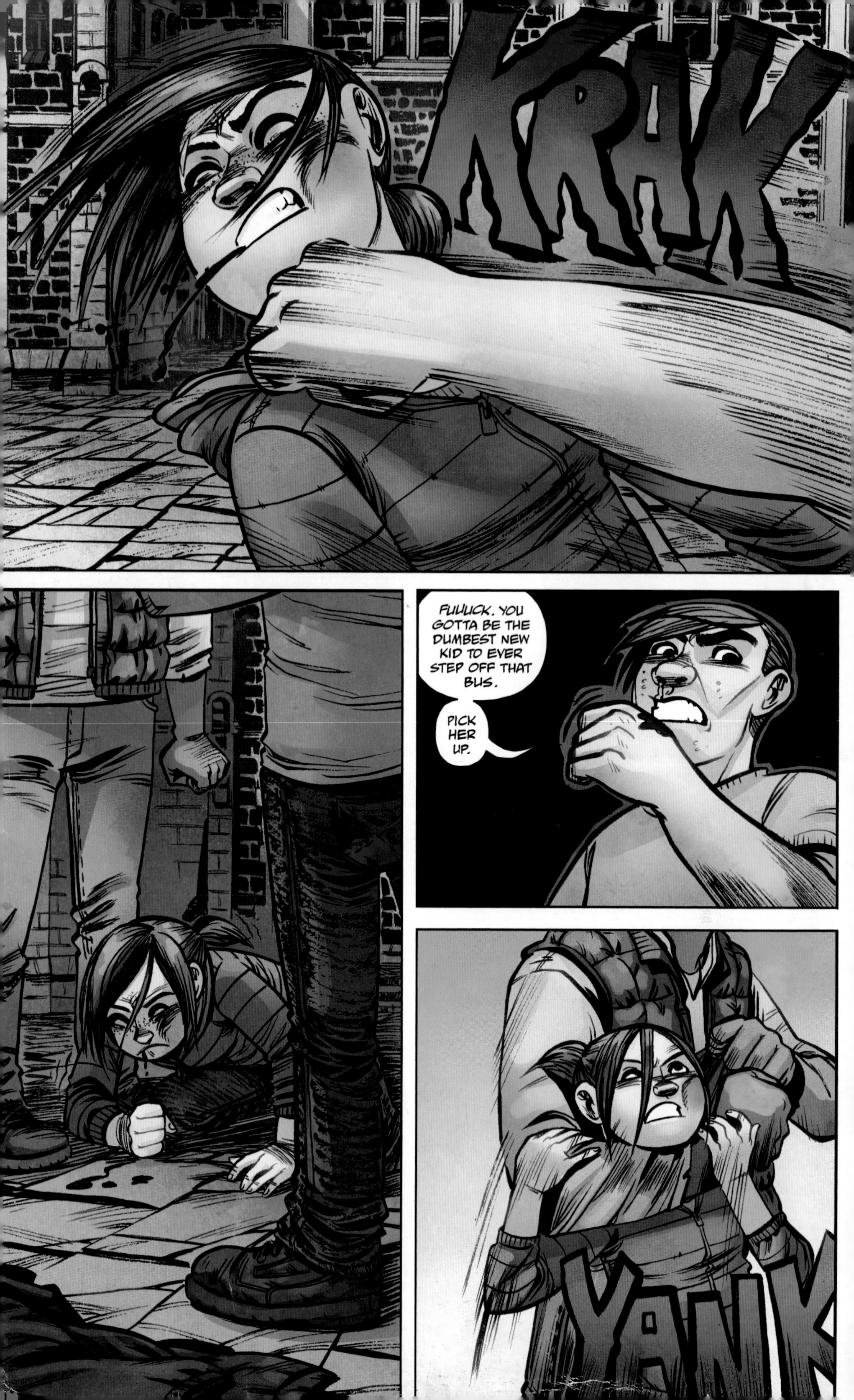
KRAK
FUUUCK. YOU GOTTA BE THE DUMBEST NEW KID TO EVER STEP OFF THAT BUS.
PICK HER UP.
YANK

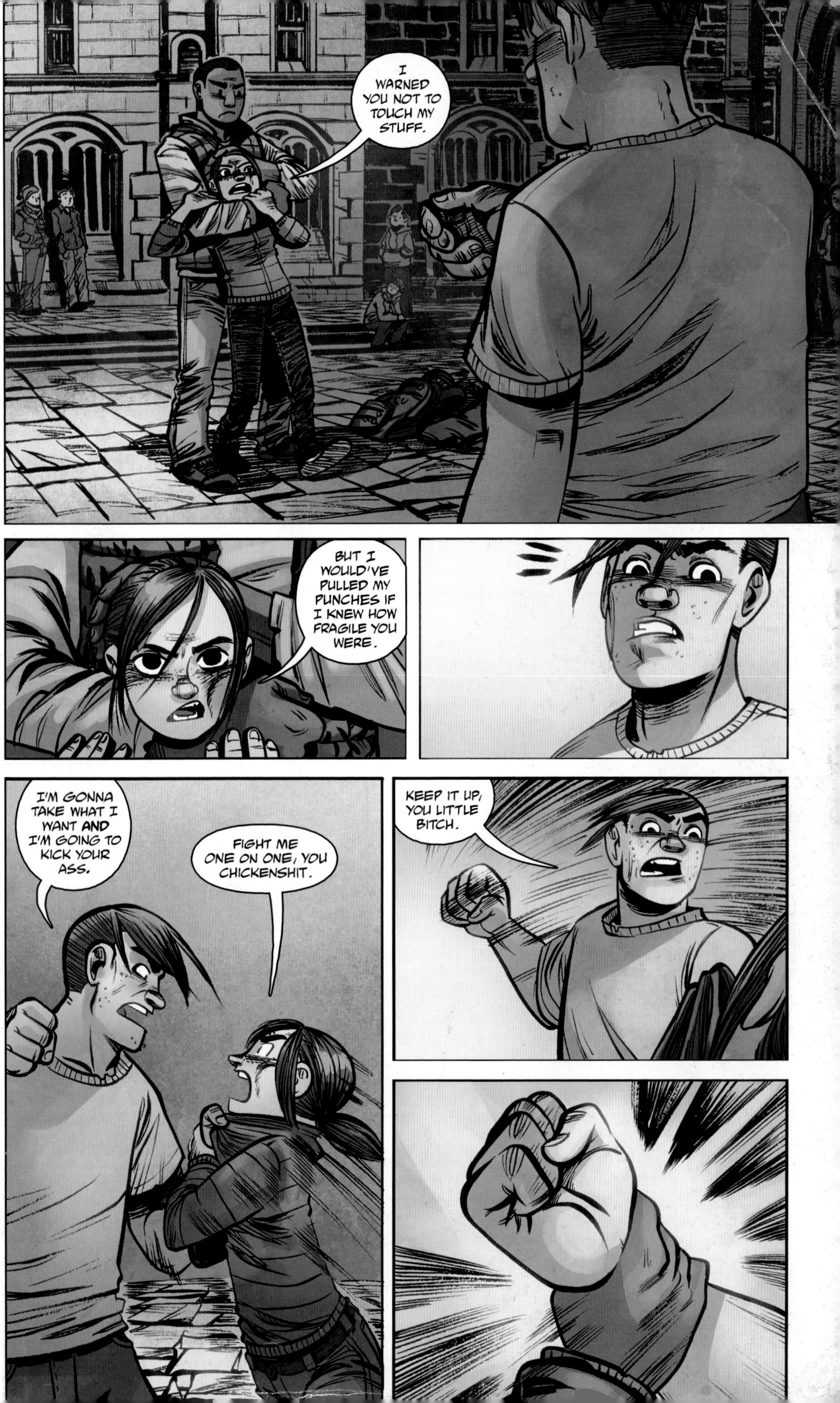
I WARNED YOU NOT TO TOUCH MY STUFF.
BUT I WOULD'VE PULLED MY PUNCHES IF I KNEW HOW FRAGILE YOU WERE.
I'M GONNA TAKE WHAT I WANT AND I'M GOING TO KICK YOUR ASS.
FIGHT ME ONE ON ONE, YOU CHICKENSHIT.
KEEP IT UP, YOU LITTLE BITCH.

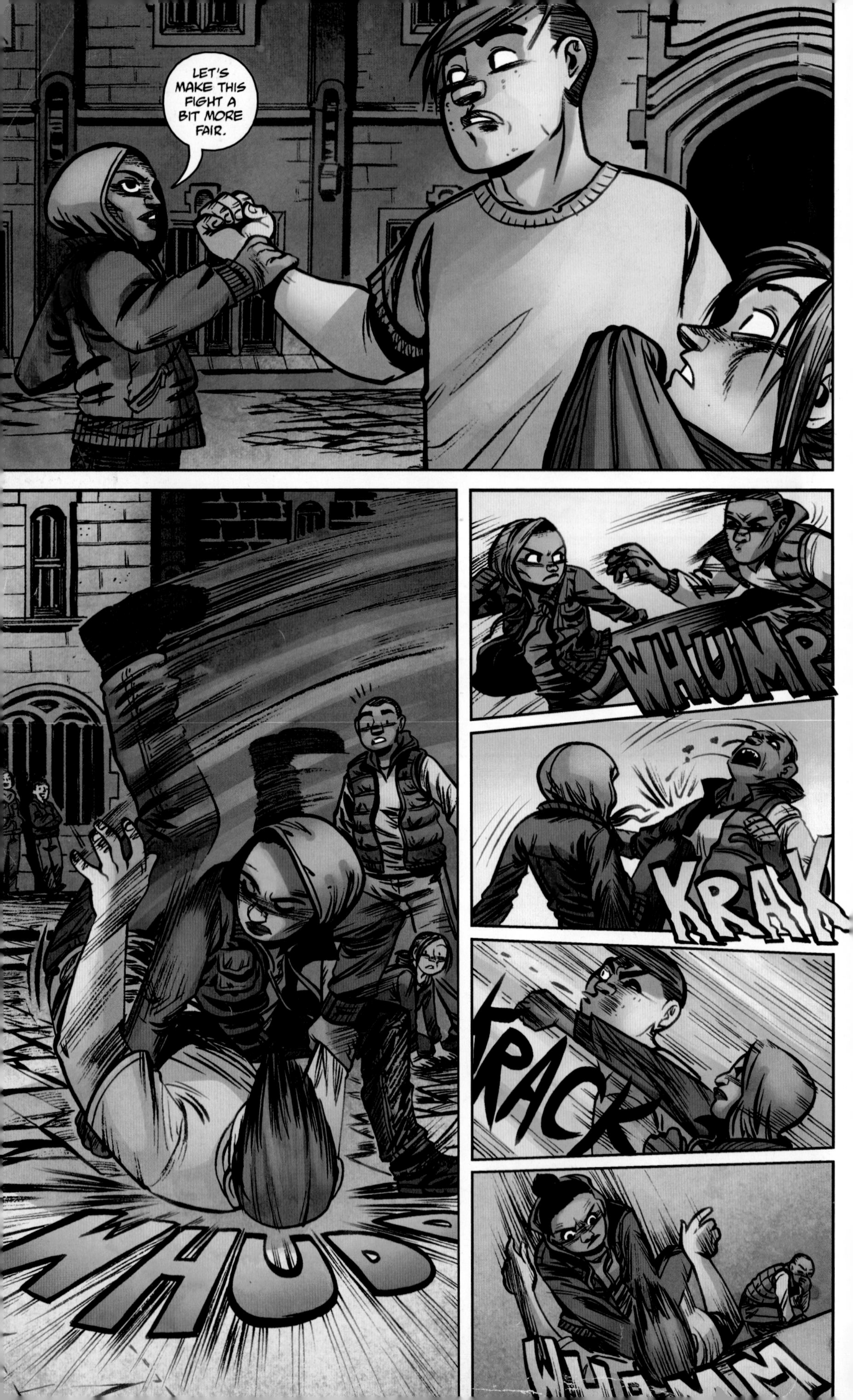
LET'S MAKE THIS FIGHT A BIT MORE FAIR.
WHUMP
KRAK

I SHOULD
STOMP YOUR
FUCKING
BALLS.

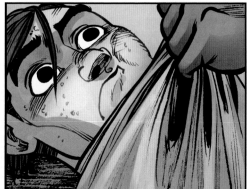

WHAT
SPECTACULAR
FUCKWADS.
WHAT'D THEY
WANT?

SOME-
THING NOT
THEIRS.

I HAD IT
COVERED.

YEAH, I
CAN SEE
THAT.

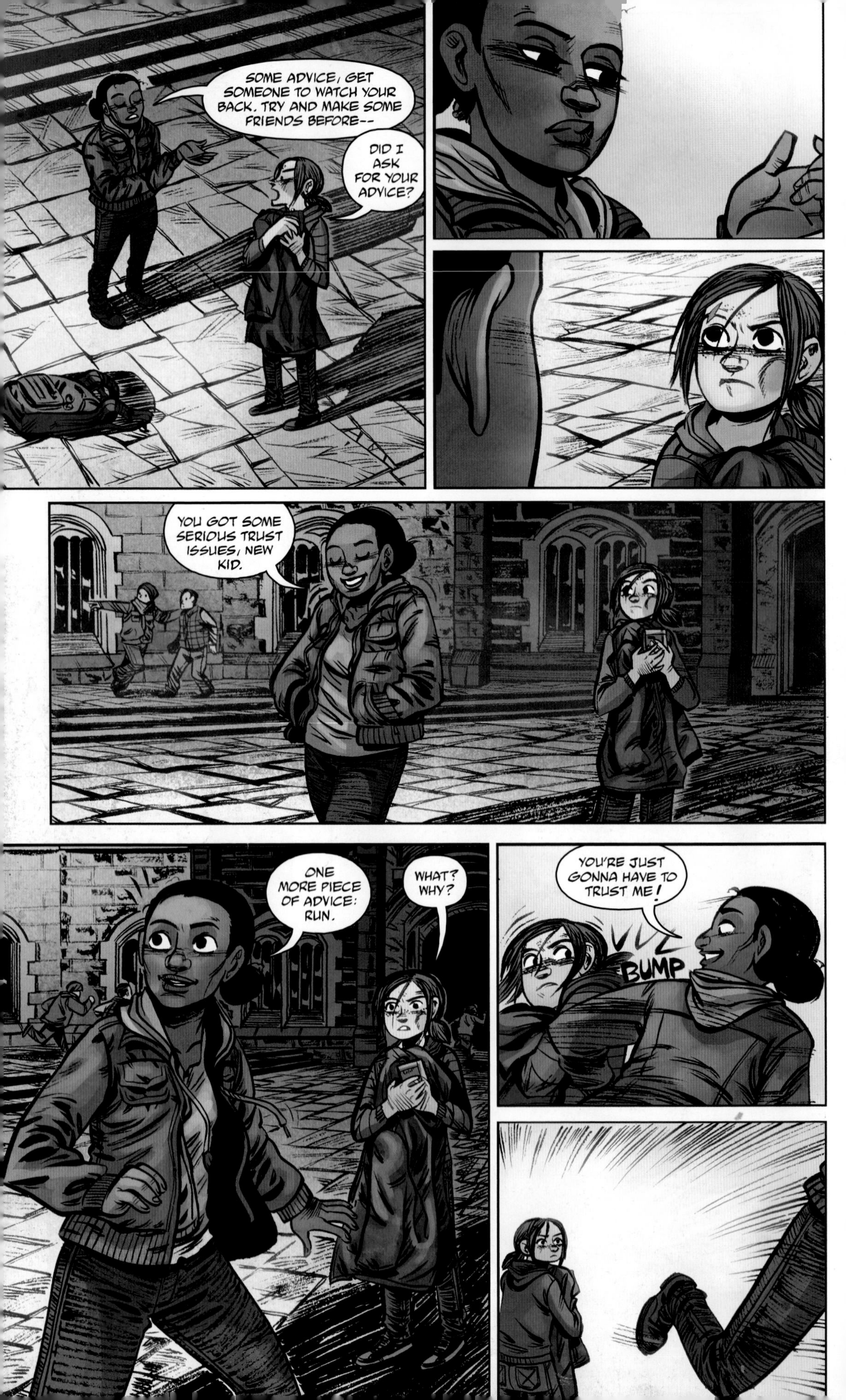
SOME ADVICE, GET SOMEONE TO WATCH YOUR BACK. TRY AND MAKE SOME FRIENDS BEFORE--
DID I ASK FOR YOUR ADVICE?
YOU GOT SOME SERIOUS TRUST ISSUES, NEW KID.
ONE MORE PIECE OF ADVICE: RUN.
WHAT? WHY?
YOU'RE JUST GONNA HAVE TO TRUST ME!
BUMP

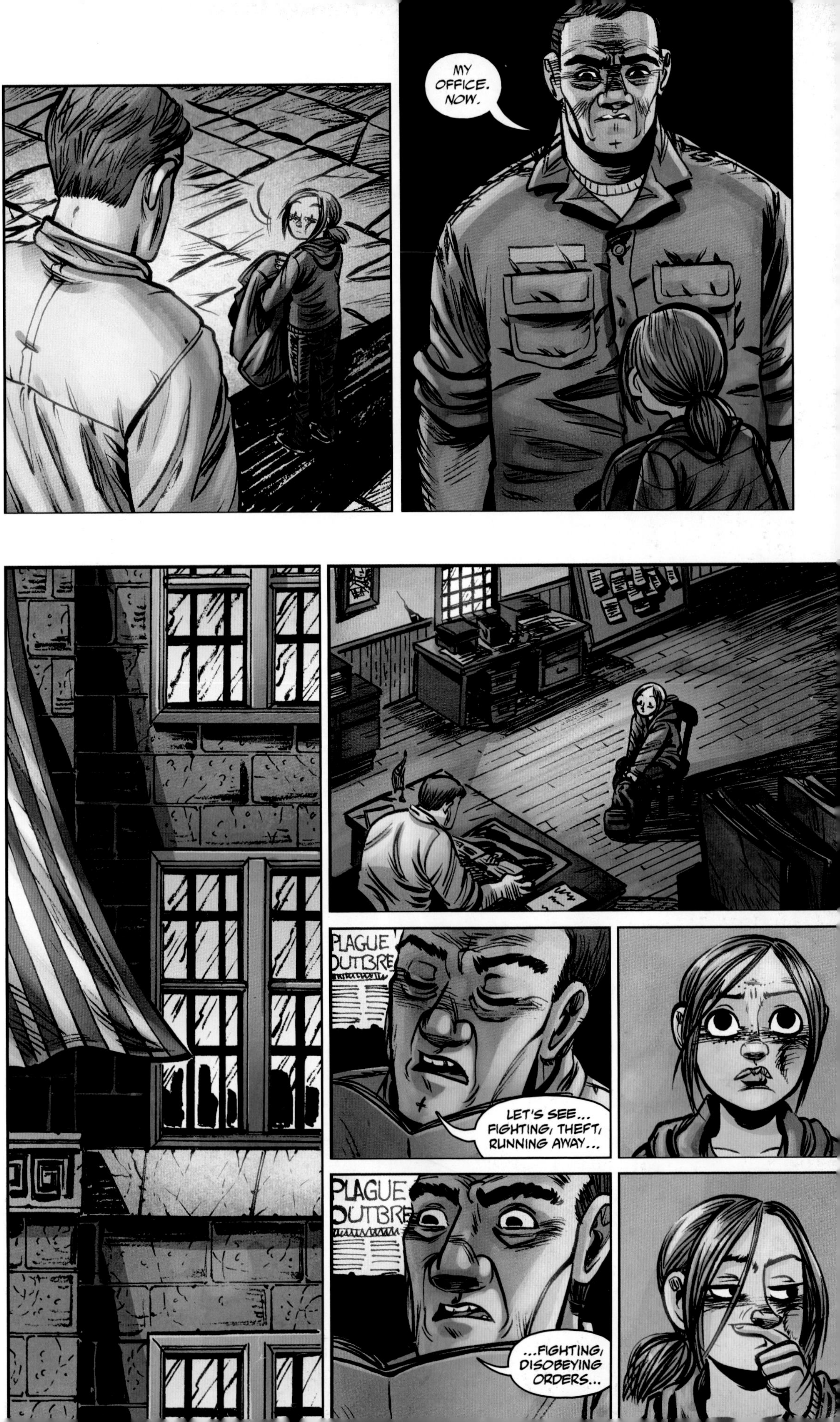
MY OFFICE. NOW.
PLAGUE OUTBRE
LET'S SEE... FIGHTING, THEFT, RUNNING AWAY...
PLAGUE OUTBRE
...FIGHTING, DISOBEYING ORDERS...

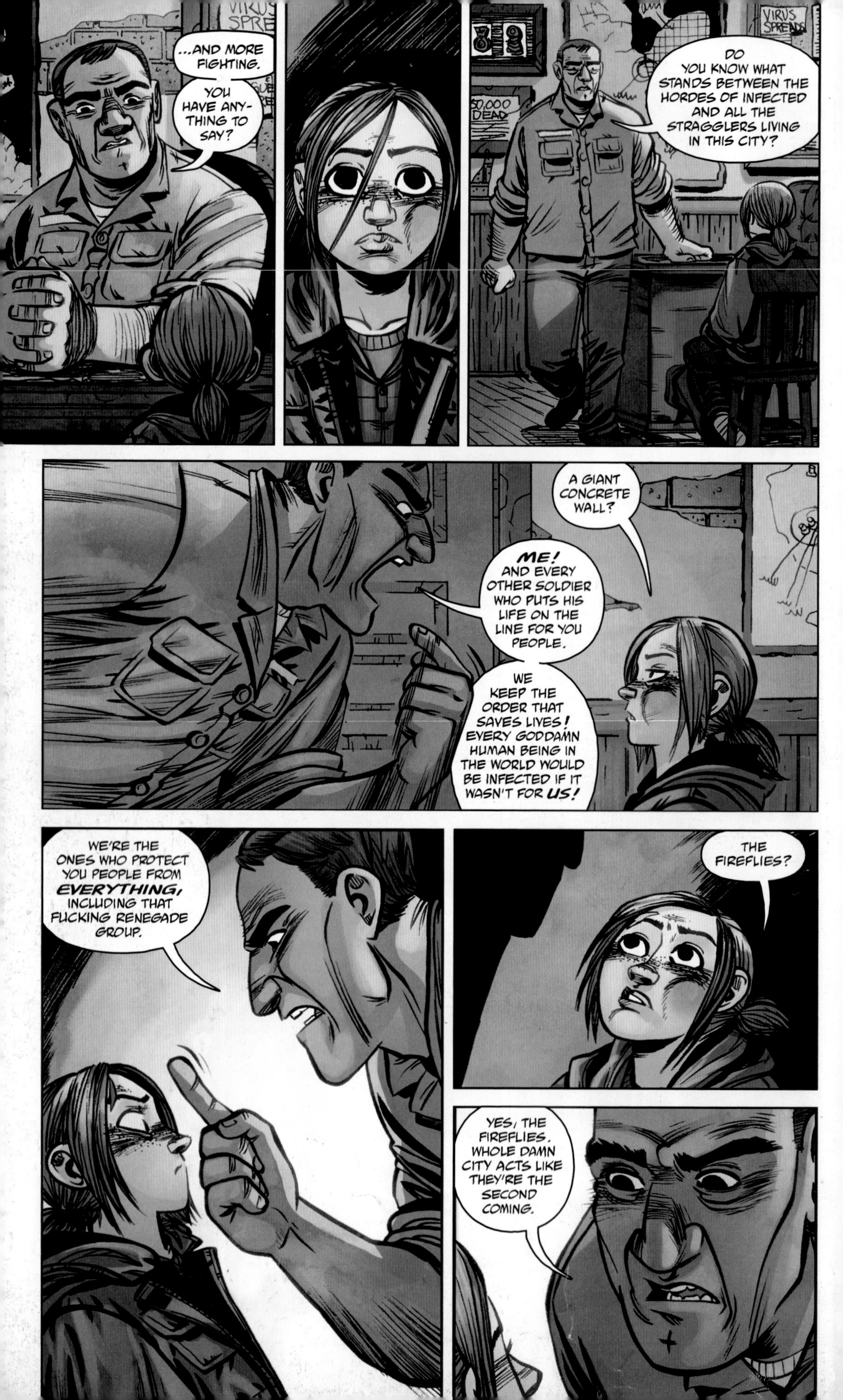

...AND MORE FIGHTING.
YOU HAVE ANYTHING TO SAY?
DO YOU KNOW WHAT STANDS BETWEEN THE HORDES OF INFECTED AND ALL THE STRAGGLERS LIVING IN THIS CITY?
A GIANT CONCRETE WALL?
ME! AND EVERY OTHER SOLDIER WHO PUTS HIS LIFE ON THE LINE FOR YOU PEOPLE.
WE KEEP THE ORDER THAT SAVES LIVES! EVERY GODDAMN HUMAN BEING IN THE WORLD WOULD BE INFECTED IF IT WASN'T FOR US!
WE'RE THE ONES WHO PROTECT YOU PEOPLE FROM EVERYTHING, INCLUDING THAT FUCKING RENEGADE GROUP.
THE FIREFLIES?
YES, THE FIREFLIES. WHOLE DAMN CITY ACTS LIKE THEY'RE THE SECOND COMING.

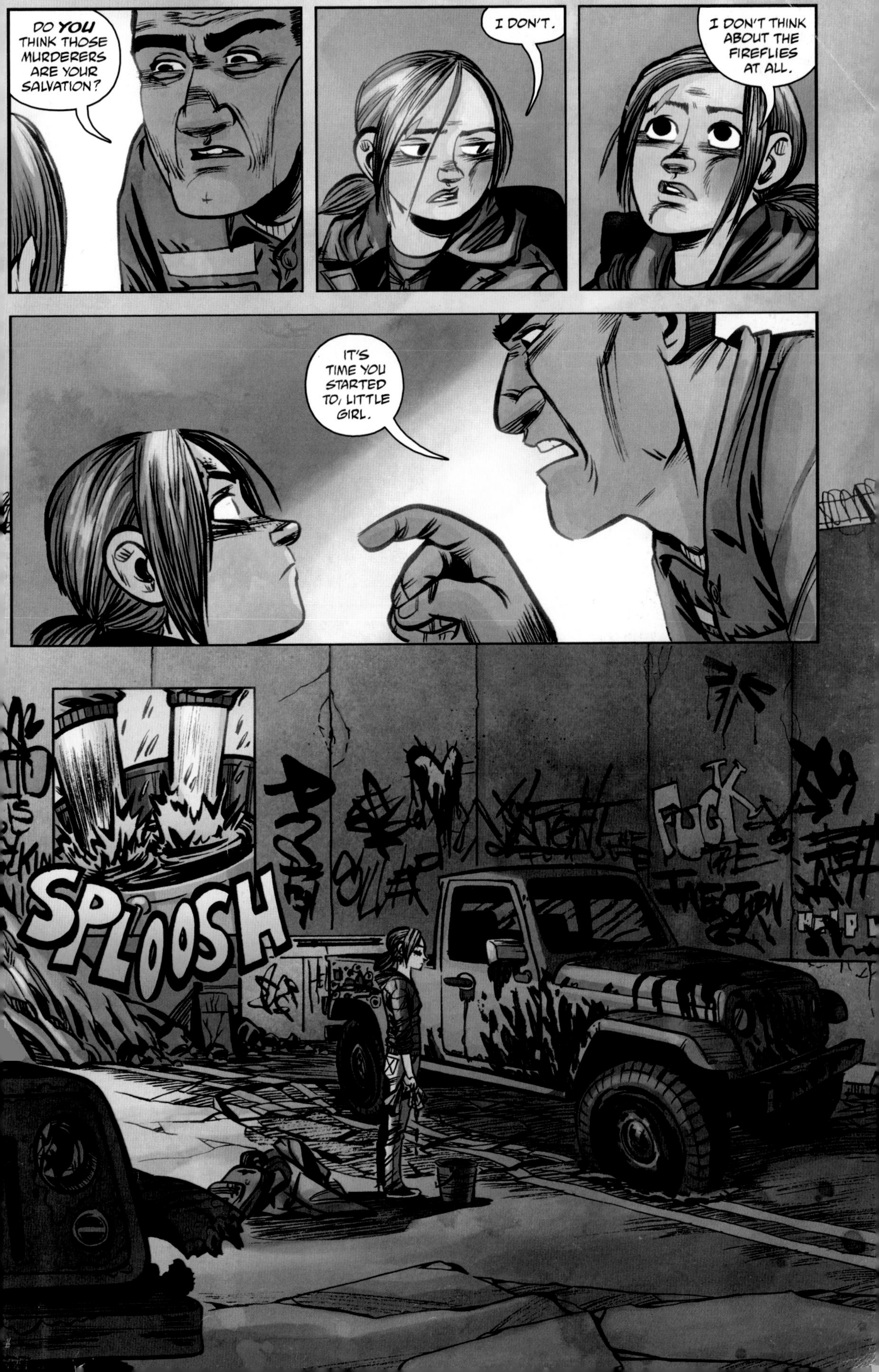
DO YOU THINK THOSE MURDERERS ARE YOUR SALVATION?
I DON'T.
I DON'T THINK ABOUT THE FIREFLIES AT ALL.
IT'S TIME YOU STARTED TO, LITTLE GIRL.
SPLOOSH
FUCK

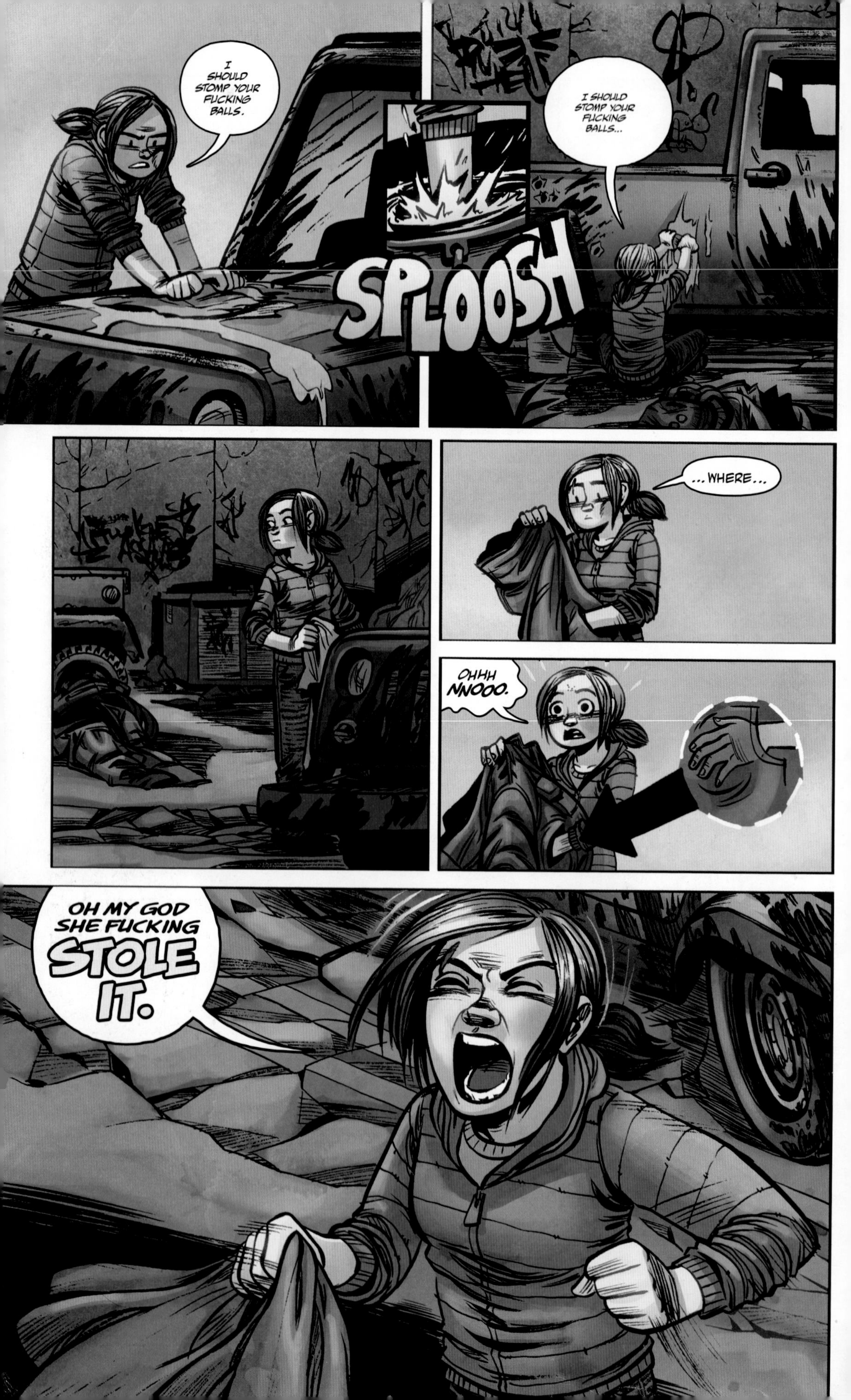
I SHOULD STOMP YOUR FUCKING BALLS.
I SHOULD STOMP YOUR FUCKING BALLS...
SPLOOSH
...WHERE...
OHHH NNOOO.
OH MY GOD SHE FUCKING STOLE IT.

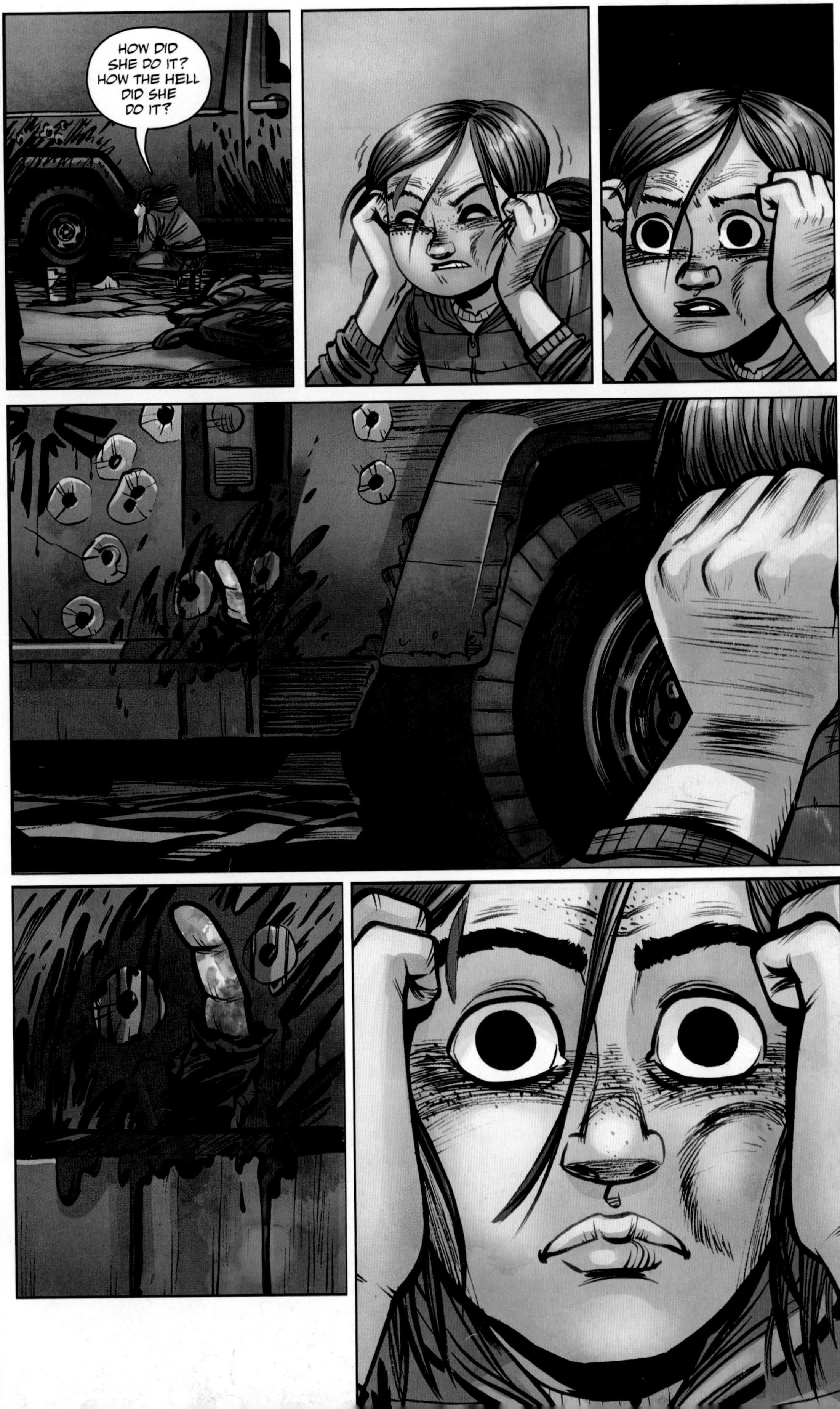
HOW DID SHE DO IT? HOW THE HELL DID SHE DO IT?

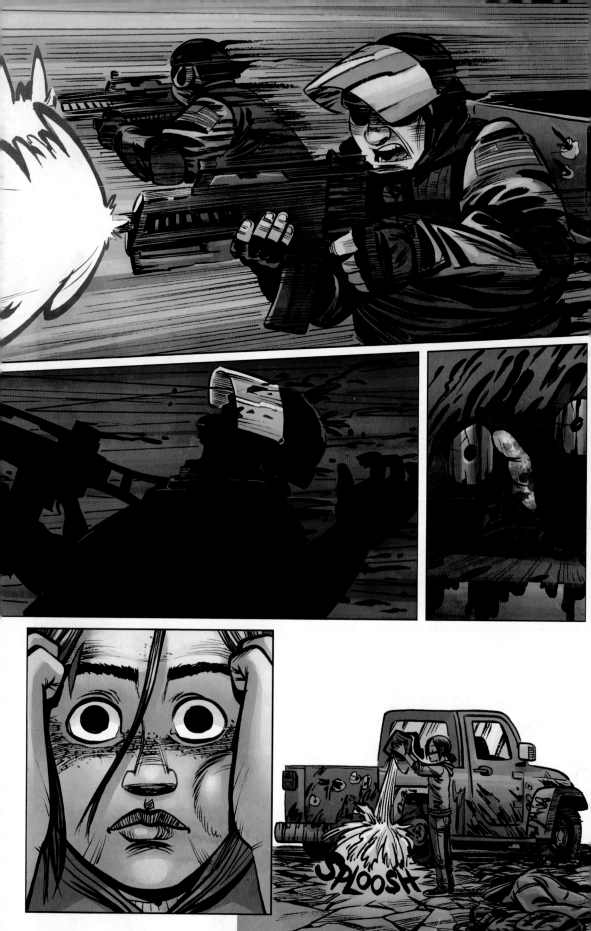

UPLOOSH

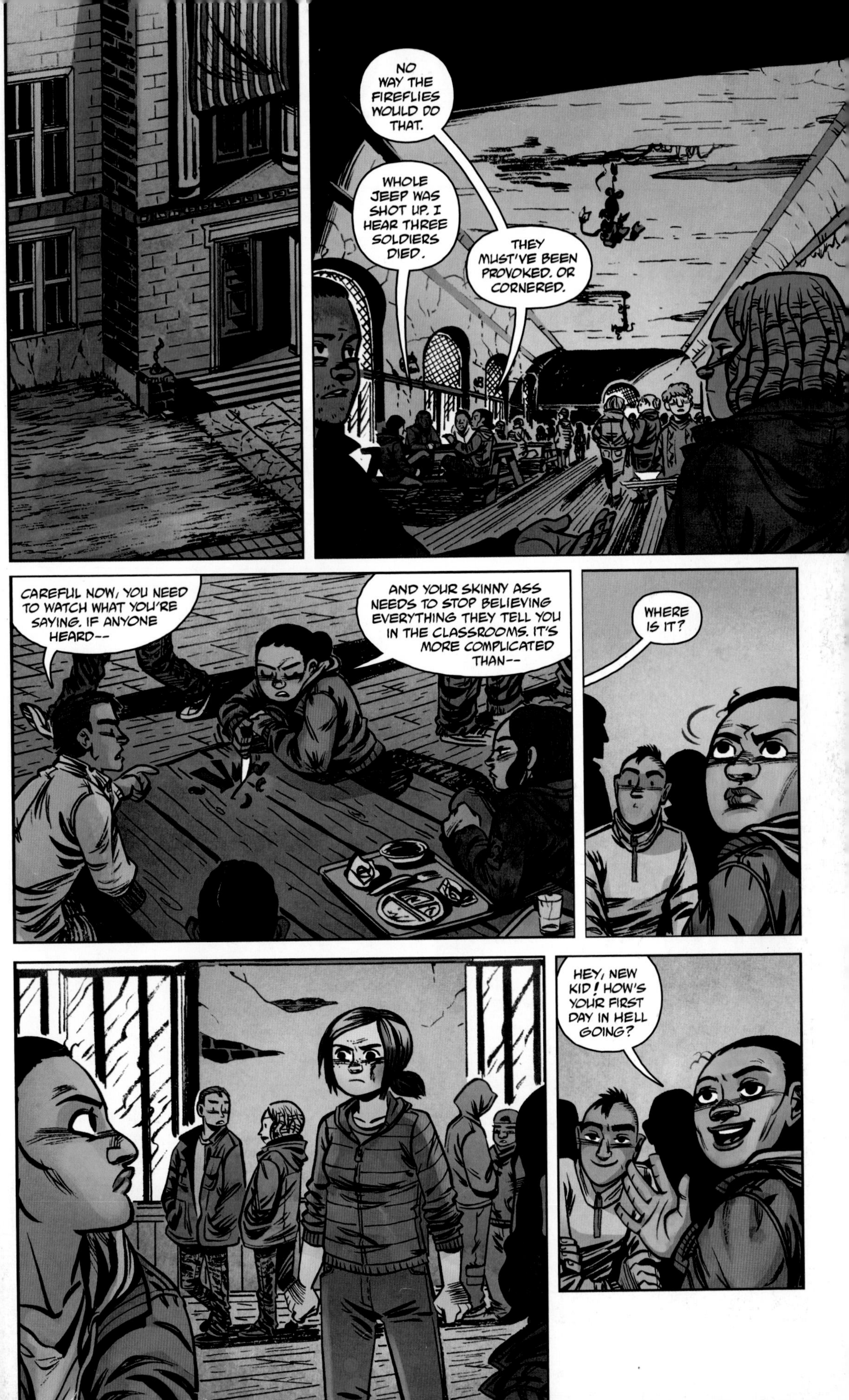
NO WAY THE FIREFLIES WOULD DO THAT.
WHOLE JEEP WAS SHOT UP. I HEAR THREE SOLDIERS DIED.
THEY MUST'VE BEEN PROVOKED. OR CORNERED.
CAREFUL NOW, YOU NEED TO WATCH WHAT YOU'RE SAYING. IF ANYONE HEARD--
AND YOUR SKINNY ASS NEEDS TO STOP BELIEVING EVERYTHING THEY TELL YOU IN THE CLASSROOMS. IT'S MORE COMPLICATED THAN--
WHERE IS IT?
HEY, NEW KID! HOW'S YOUR FIRST DAY IN HELL GOING?

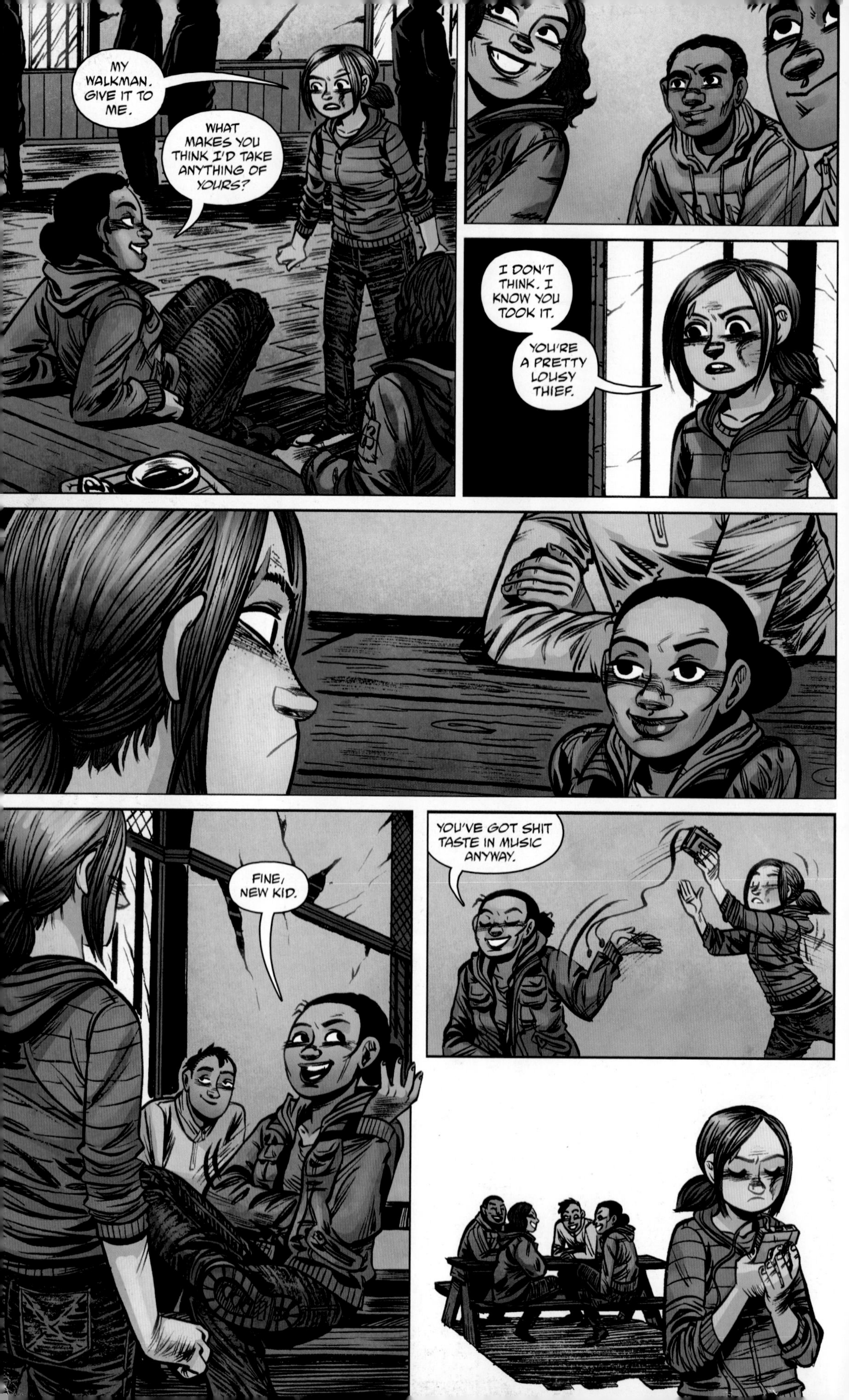

MY WALKMAN. GIVE IT TO ME.
WHAT MAKES YOU THINK I'D TAKE ANYTHING OF YOURS?
I DON'T THINK. I KNOW YOU TOOK IT.
YOU'RE A PRETTY LOUSY THIEF.
FINE, NEW KID.
YOU'VE GOT SHIT TASTE IN MUSIC ANYWAY.

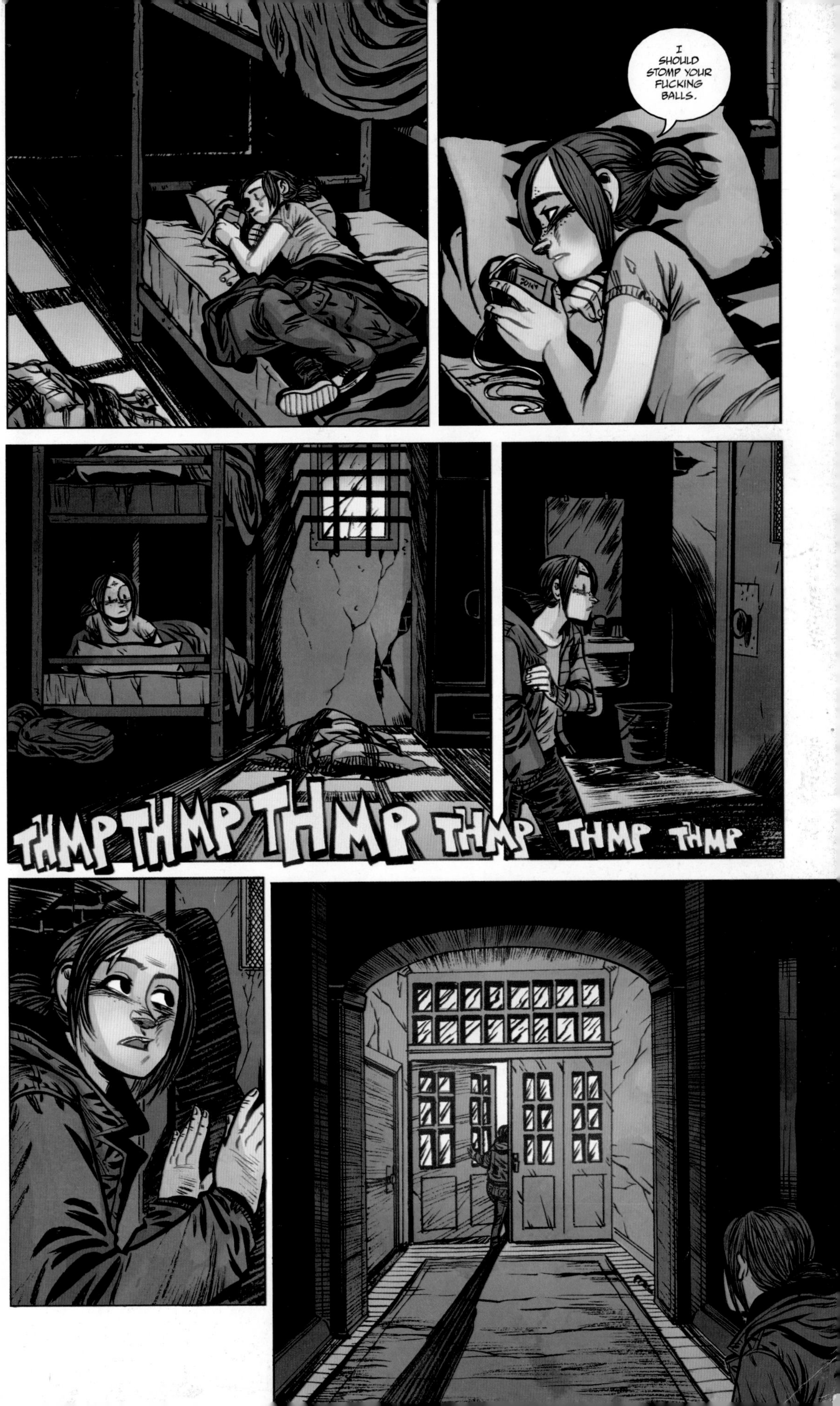
I SHOULD STOMP YOUR FUCKING BALLS.
THMP THMP THMP THMP THMP THMP

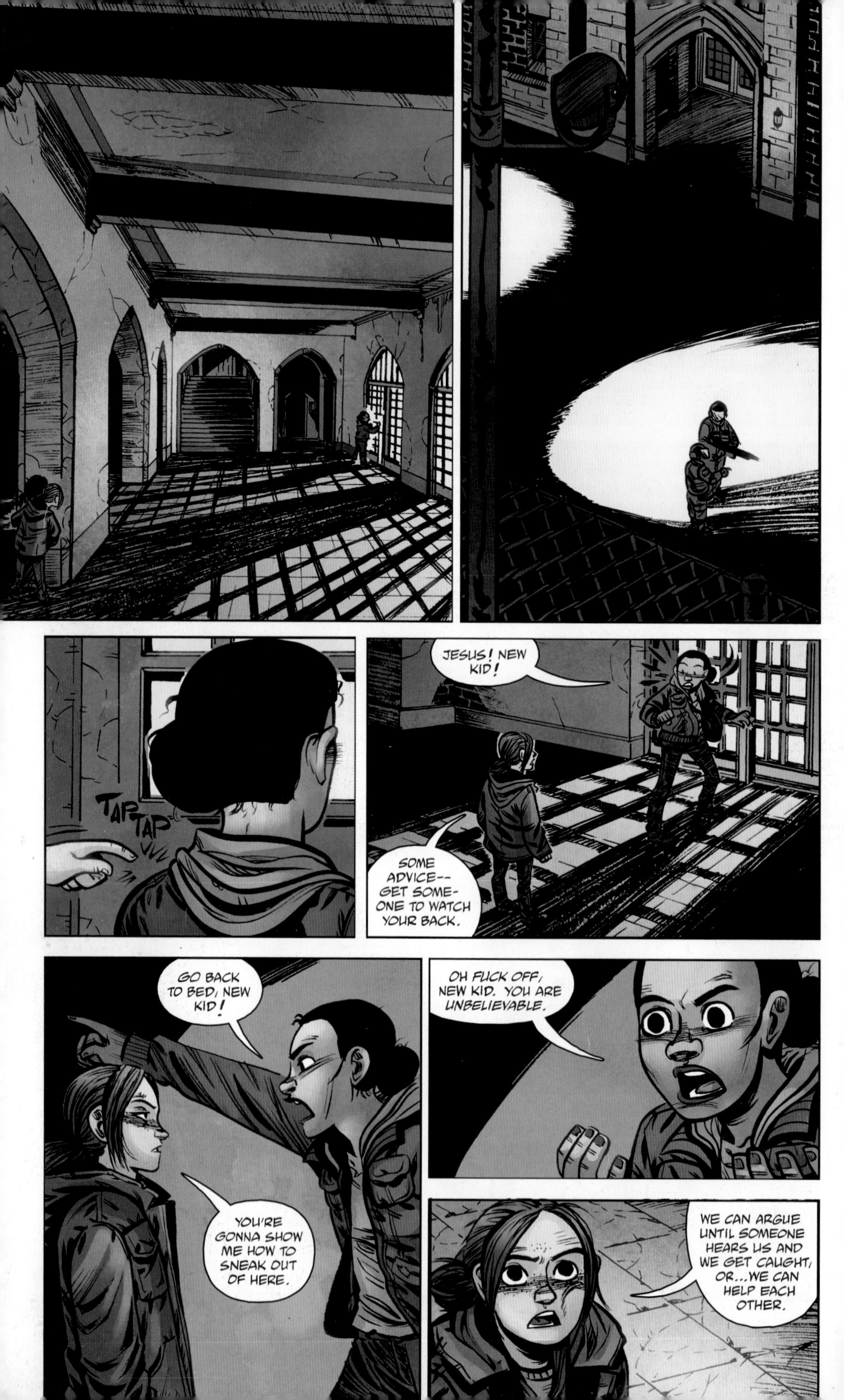
TAP TAP
JESUS! NEW KID!
SOME ADVICE-- GET SOME-ONE TO WATCH YOUR BACK.
GO BACK TO BED, NEW KID!
OH FUCK OFF, NEW KID. YOU ARE UNBELIEVABLE.
YOU'RE GONNA SHOW ME HOW TO SNEAK OUT OF HERE.
WE CAN ARGUE UNTIL SOMEONE HEARS US AND WE GET CAUGHT, OR...WE CAN HELP EACH OTHER.

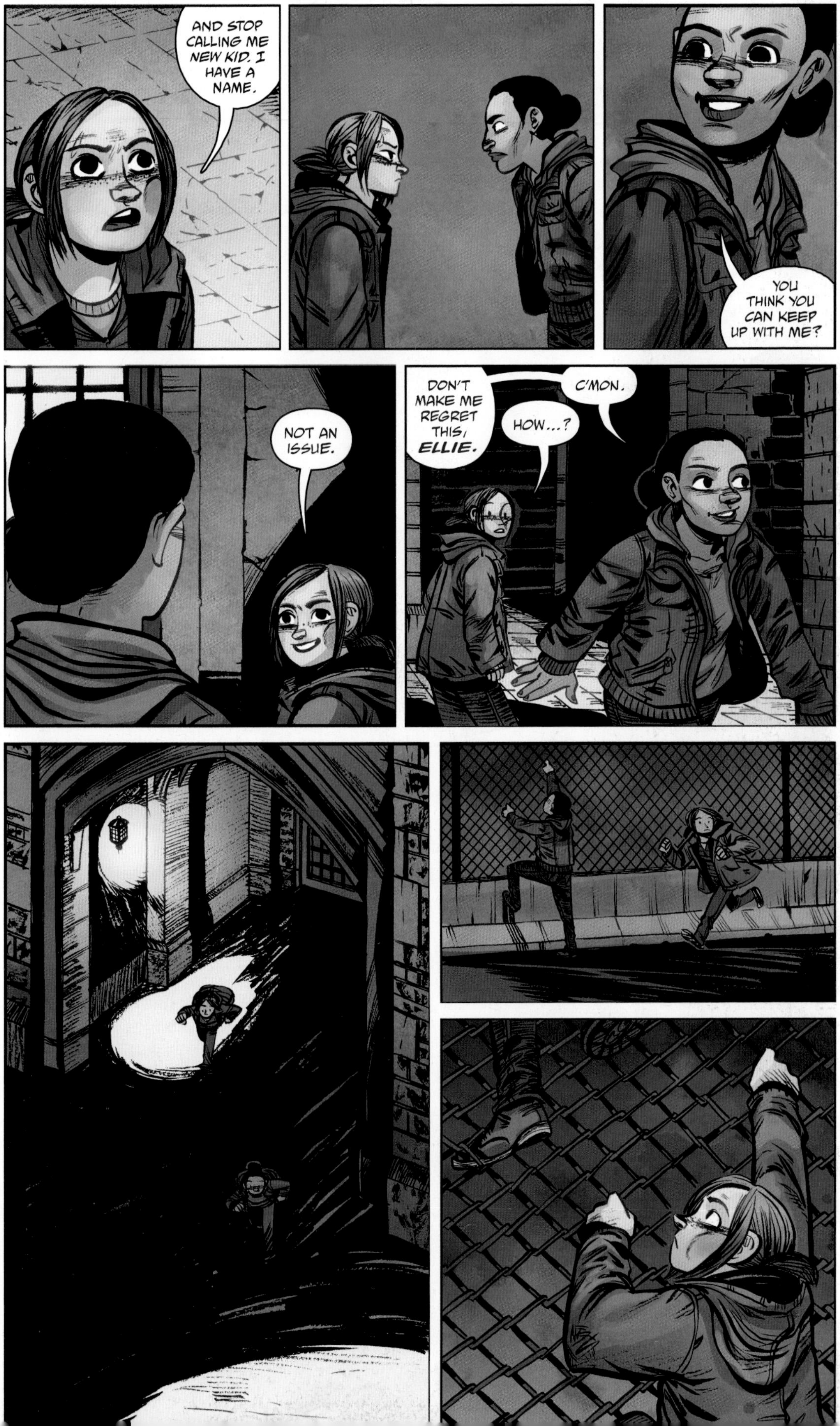
AND STOP CALLING ME NEW KID. I HAVE A NAME.
YOU THINK YOU CAN KEEP UP WITH ME?
NOT AN ISSUE.
DON'T MAKE ME REGRET THIS, ELLIE.
C'MON.
HOW...?

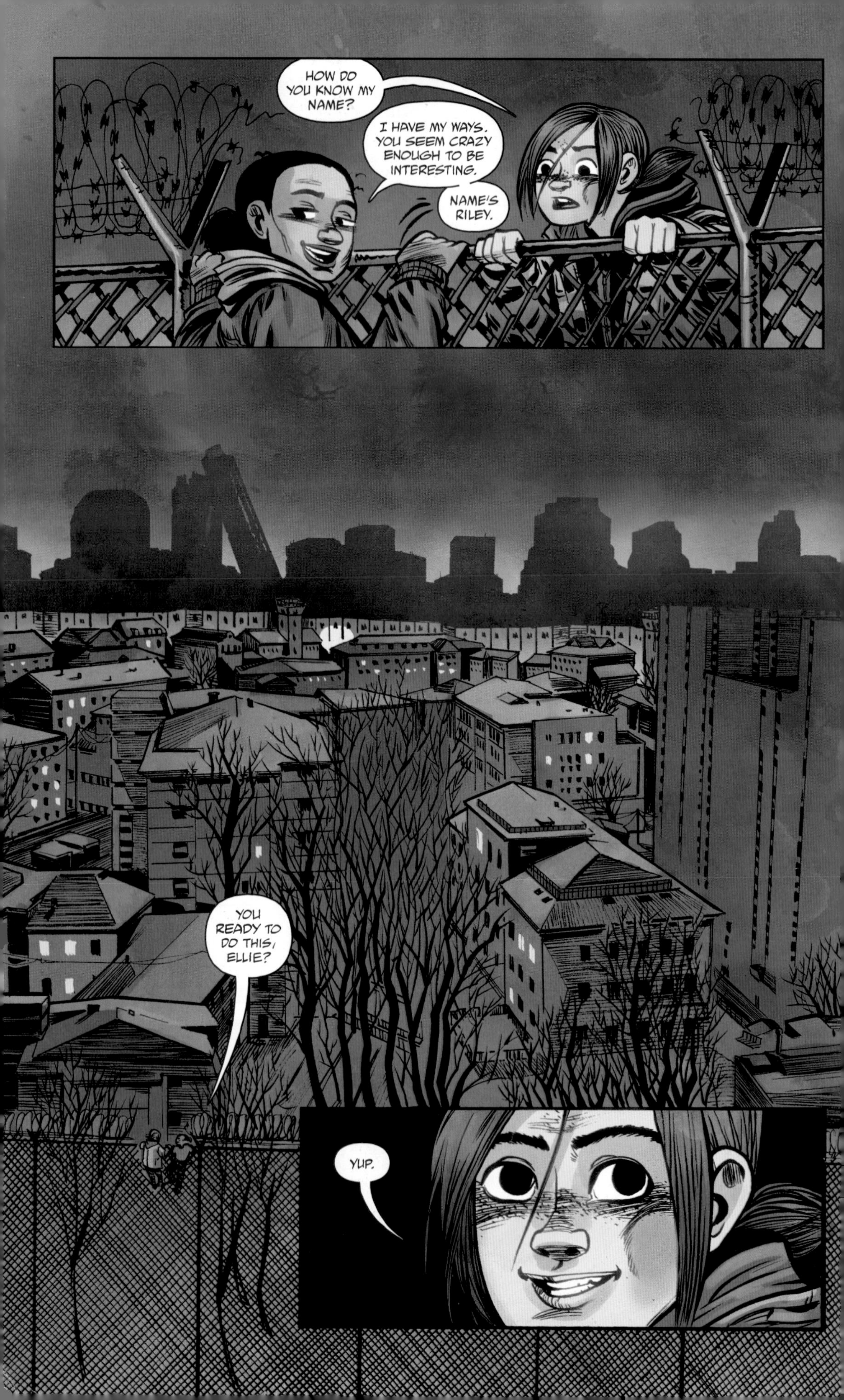
HOW DO YOU KNOW MY NAME?
I HAVE MY WAYS. YOU SEEM CRAZY ENOUGH TO BE INTERESTING.
NAME'S RILEY.
YOU READY TO DO THIS, ELLIE?
YUP.

CHAPTER TWO

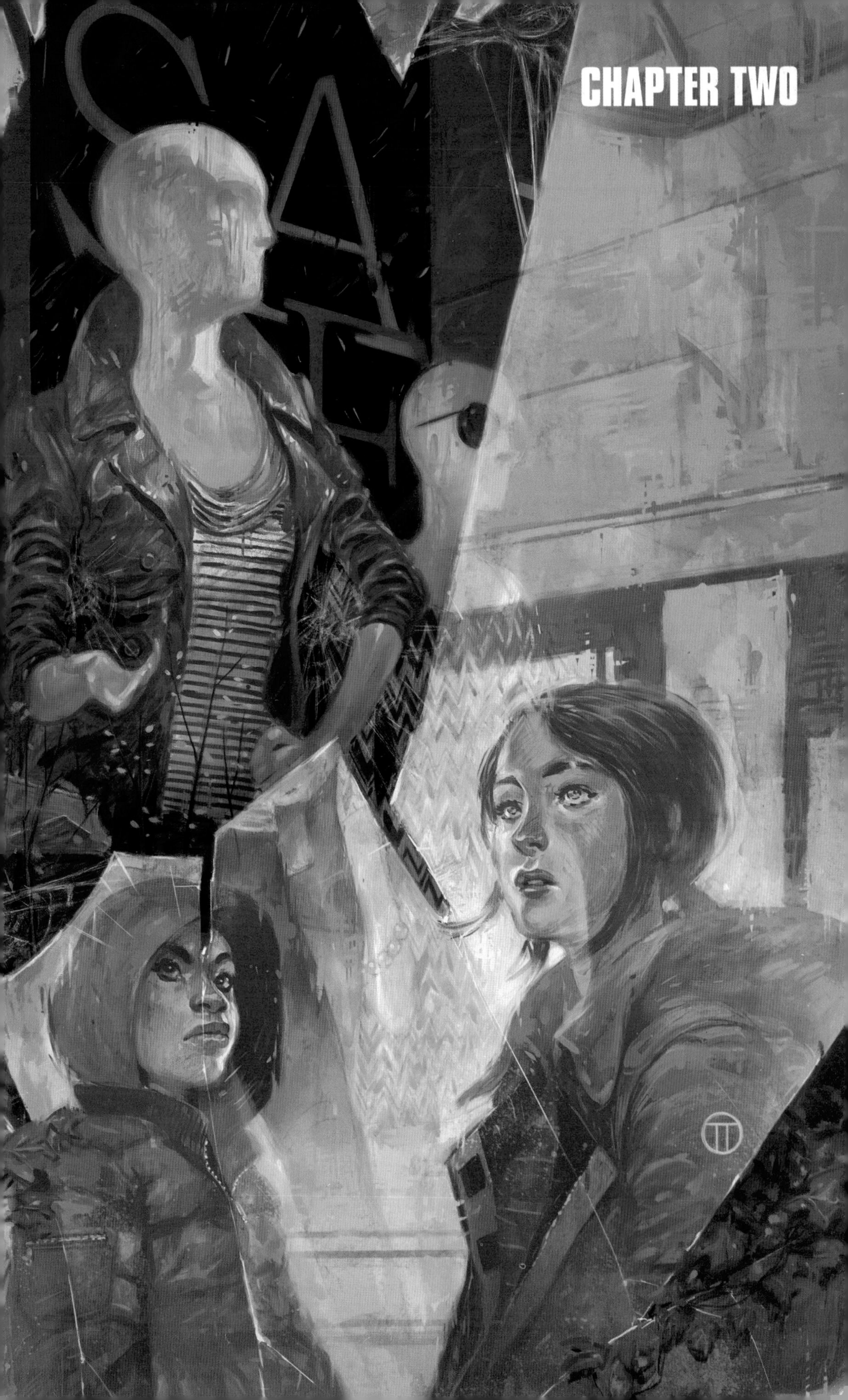

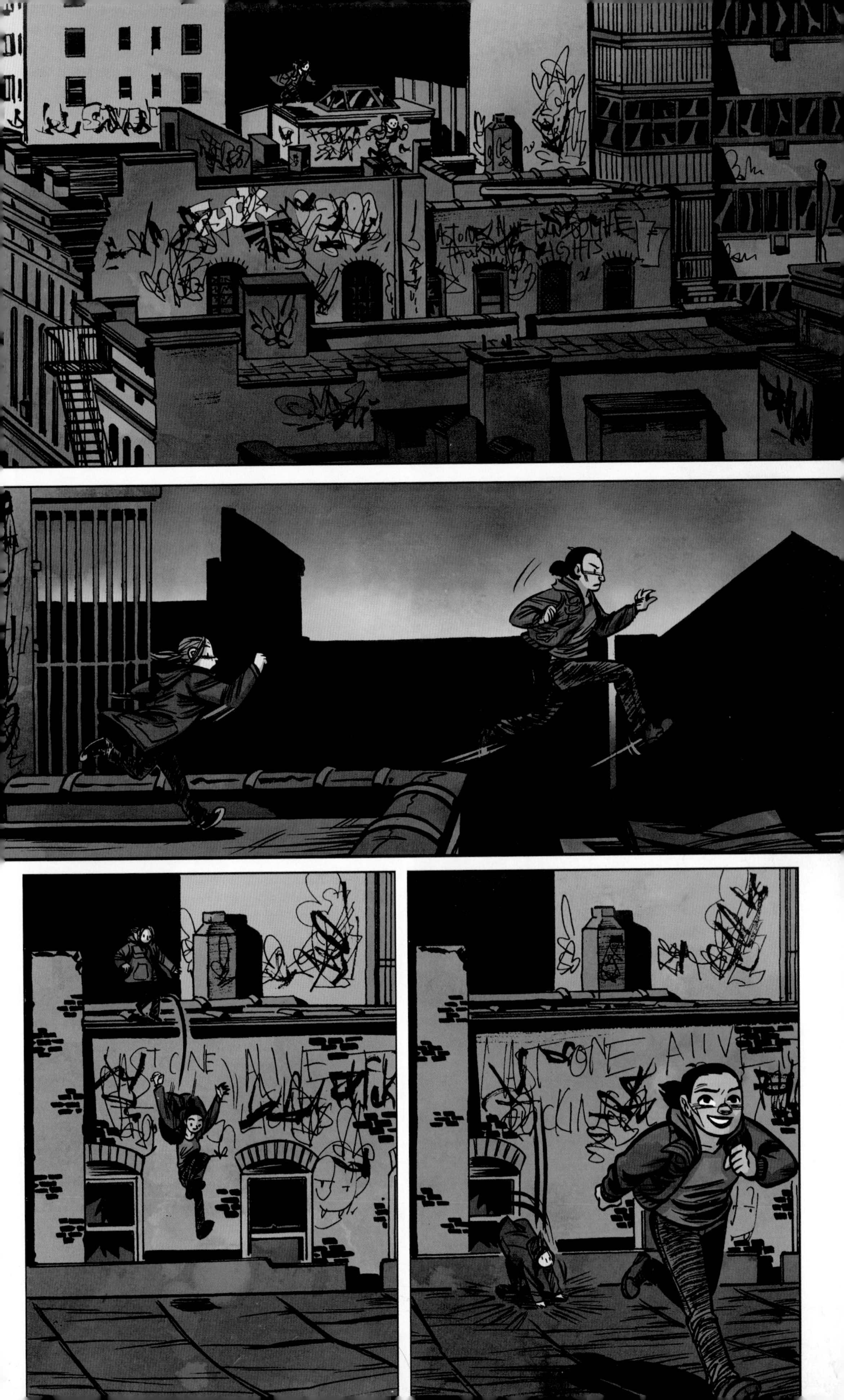

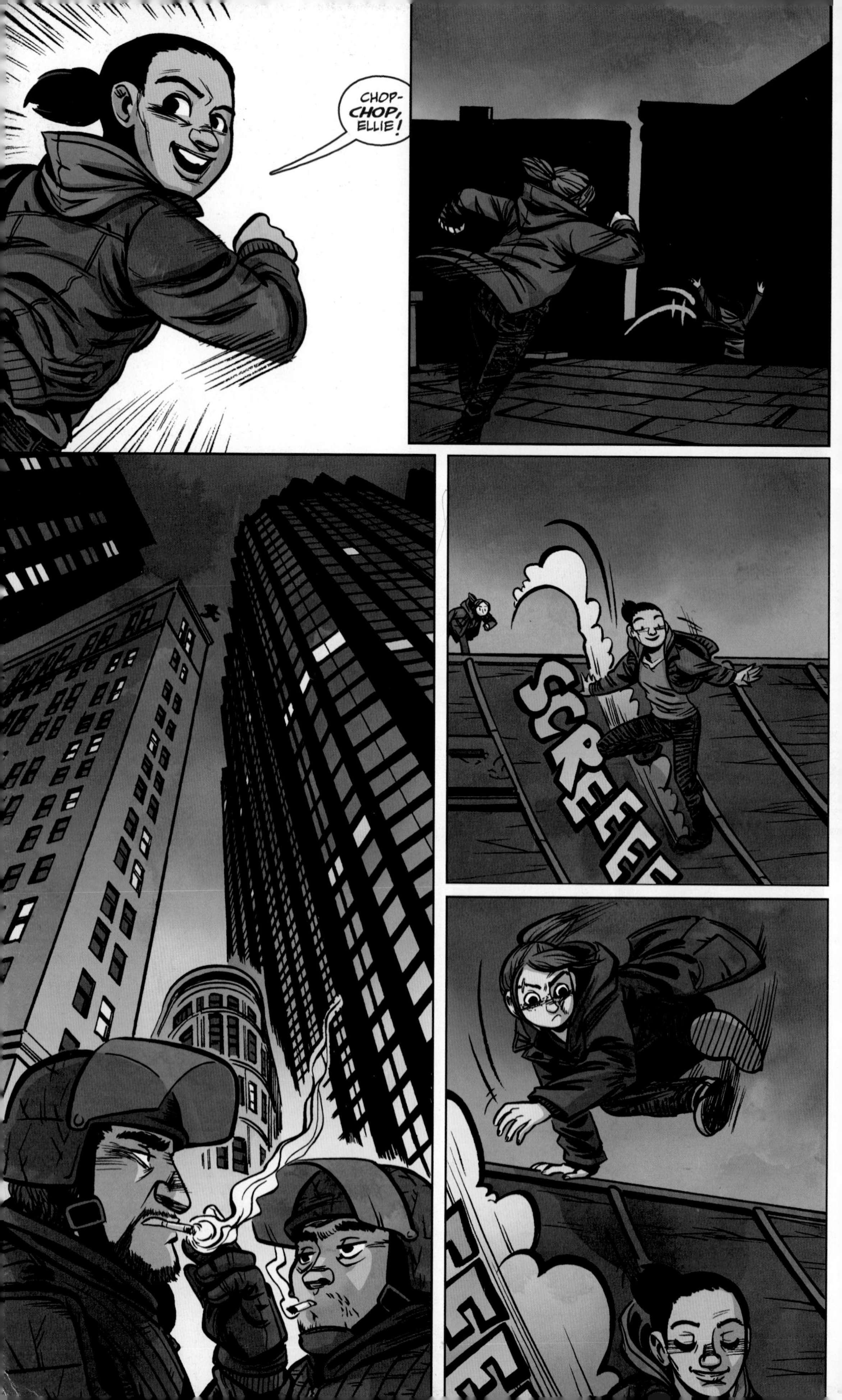
CHOP-CHOP, ELLIE!
SCREEEE

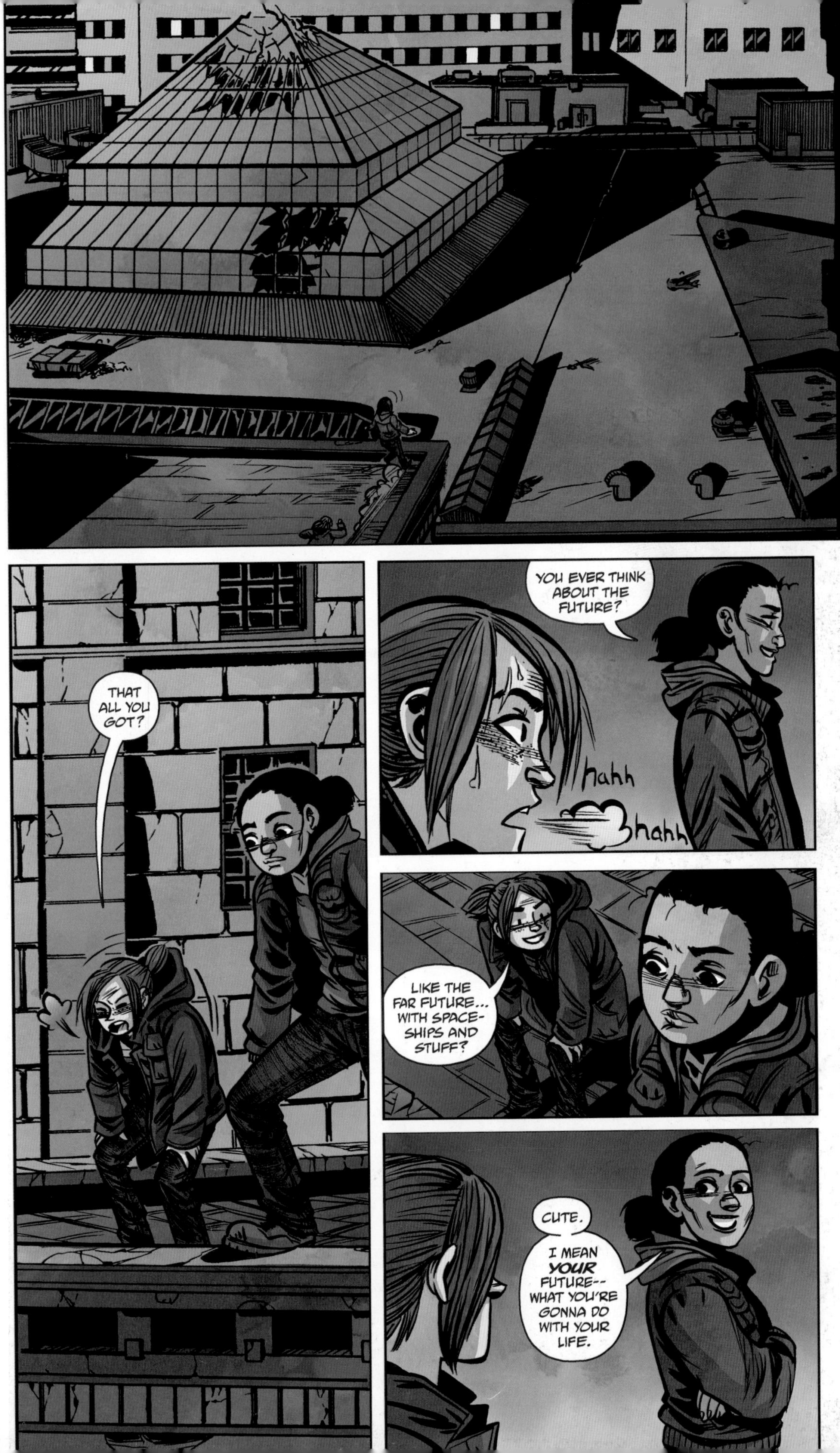
THAT ALL YOU GOT?
YOU EVER THINK ABOUT THE FUTURE?
hahh
hahh
LIKE THE FAR FUTURE... WITH SPACE-SHIPS AND STUFF?
CUTE.
I MEAN YOUR FUTURE-- WHAT YOU'RE GONNA DO WITH YOUR LIFE.

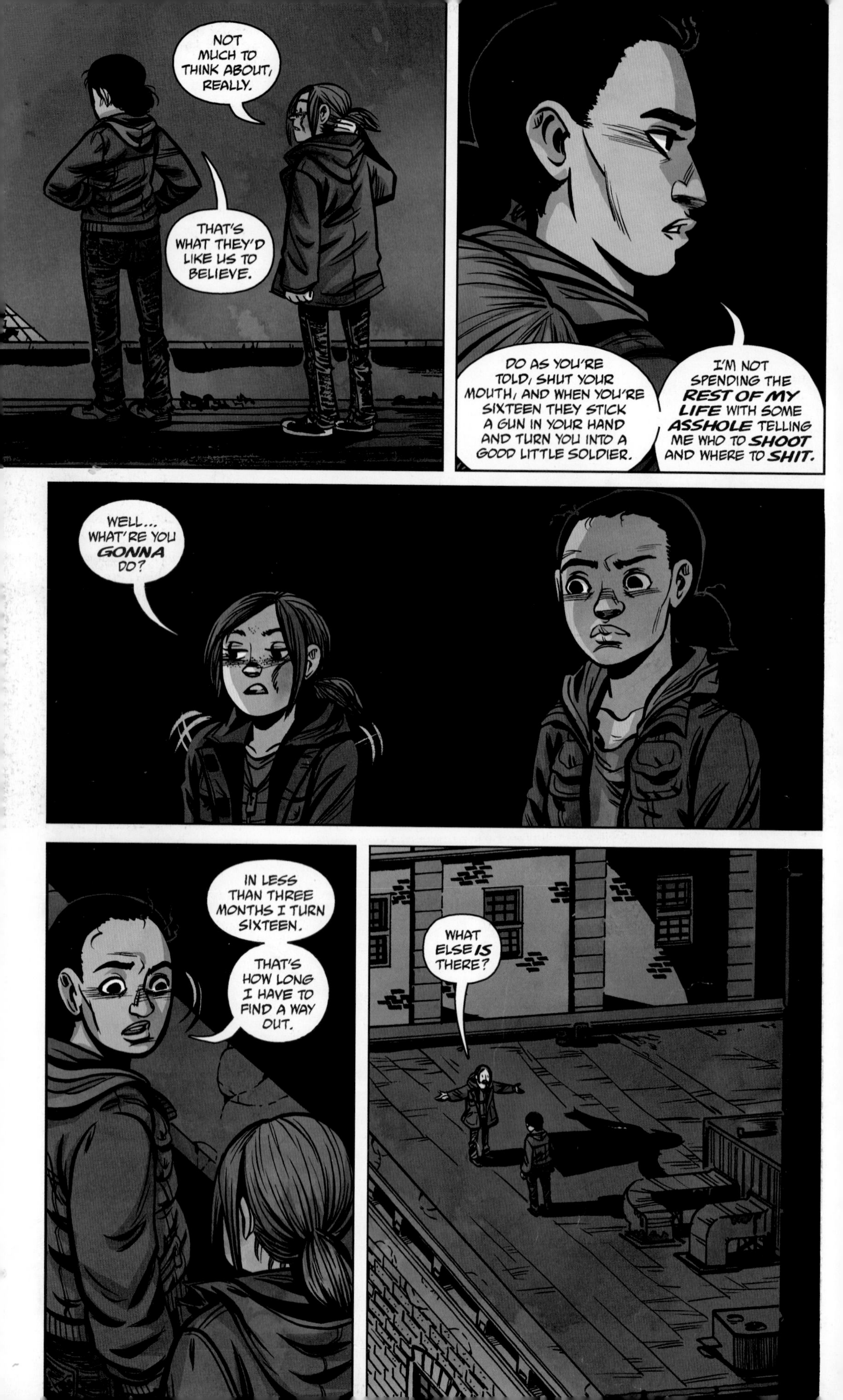
NOT MUCH TO THINK ABOUT, REALLY.
THAT'S WHAT THEY'D LIKE US TO BELIEVE.
DO AS YOU'RE TOLD, SHUT YOUR MOUTH, AND WHEN YOU'RE SIXTEEN THEY STICK A GUN IN YOUR HAND AND TURN YOU INTO A GOOD LITTLE SOLDIER.
I'M NOT SPENDING THE REST OF MY LIFE WITH SOME ASSHOLE TELLING ME WHO TO SHOOT AND WHERE TO SHIT.
WELL... WHAT'RE YOU GONNA DO?
IN LESS THAN THREE MONTHS I TURN SIXTEEN.
THAT'S HOW LONG I HAVE TO FIND A WAY OUT.
WHAT ELSE IS THERE?

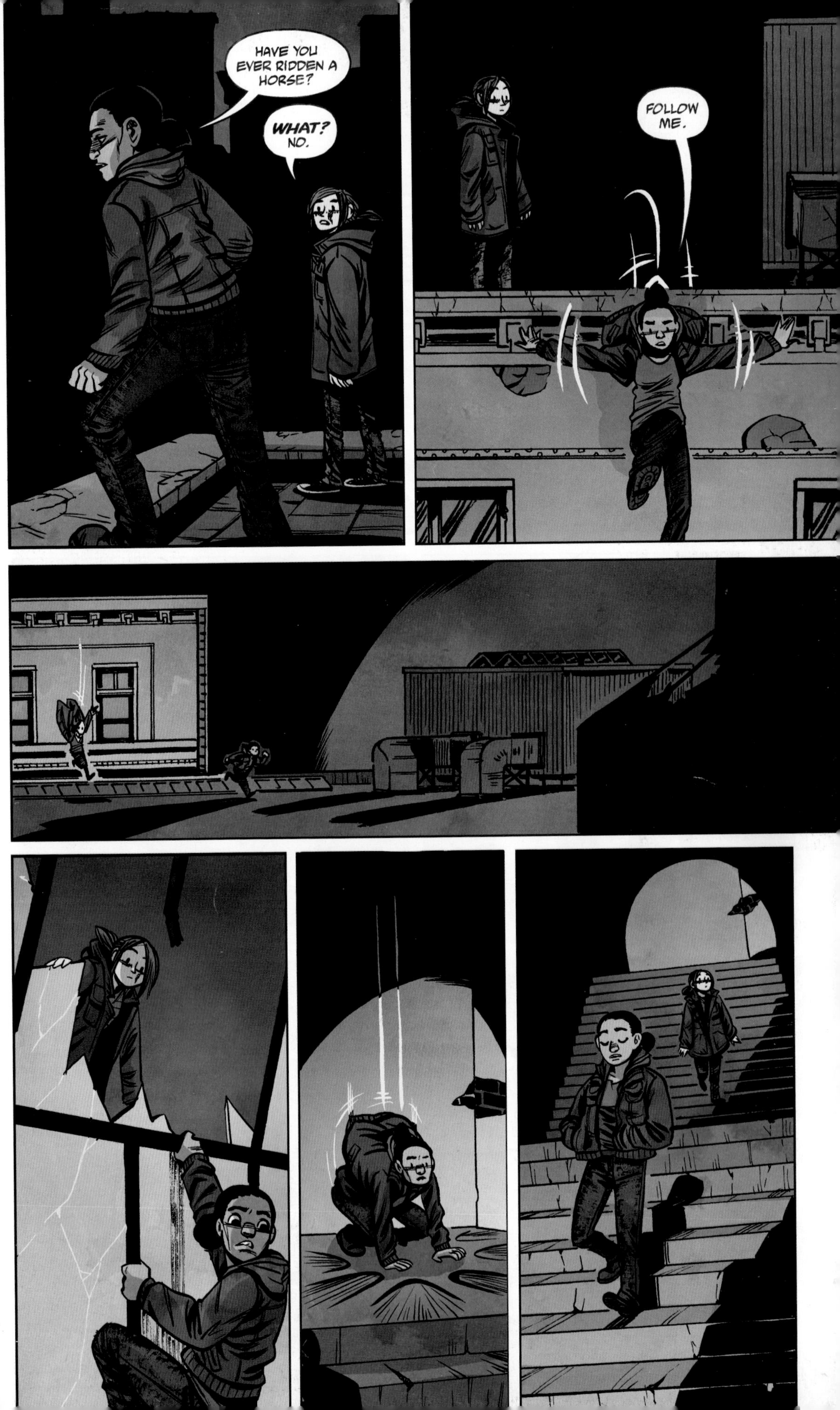

HAVE YOU EVER RIDDEN A HORSE?
WHAT? NO.
FOLLOW ME.

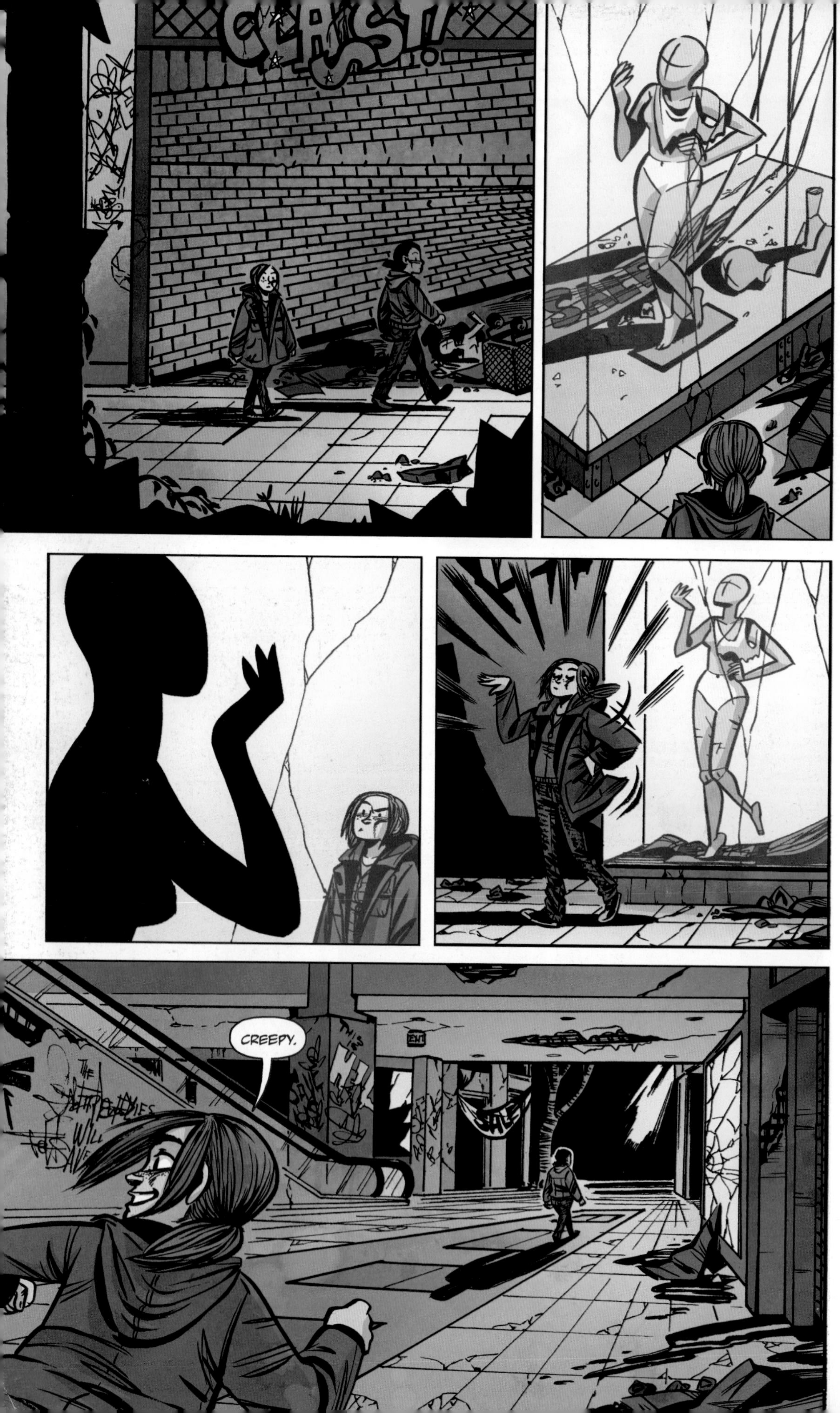
CREEPY.

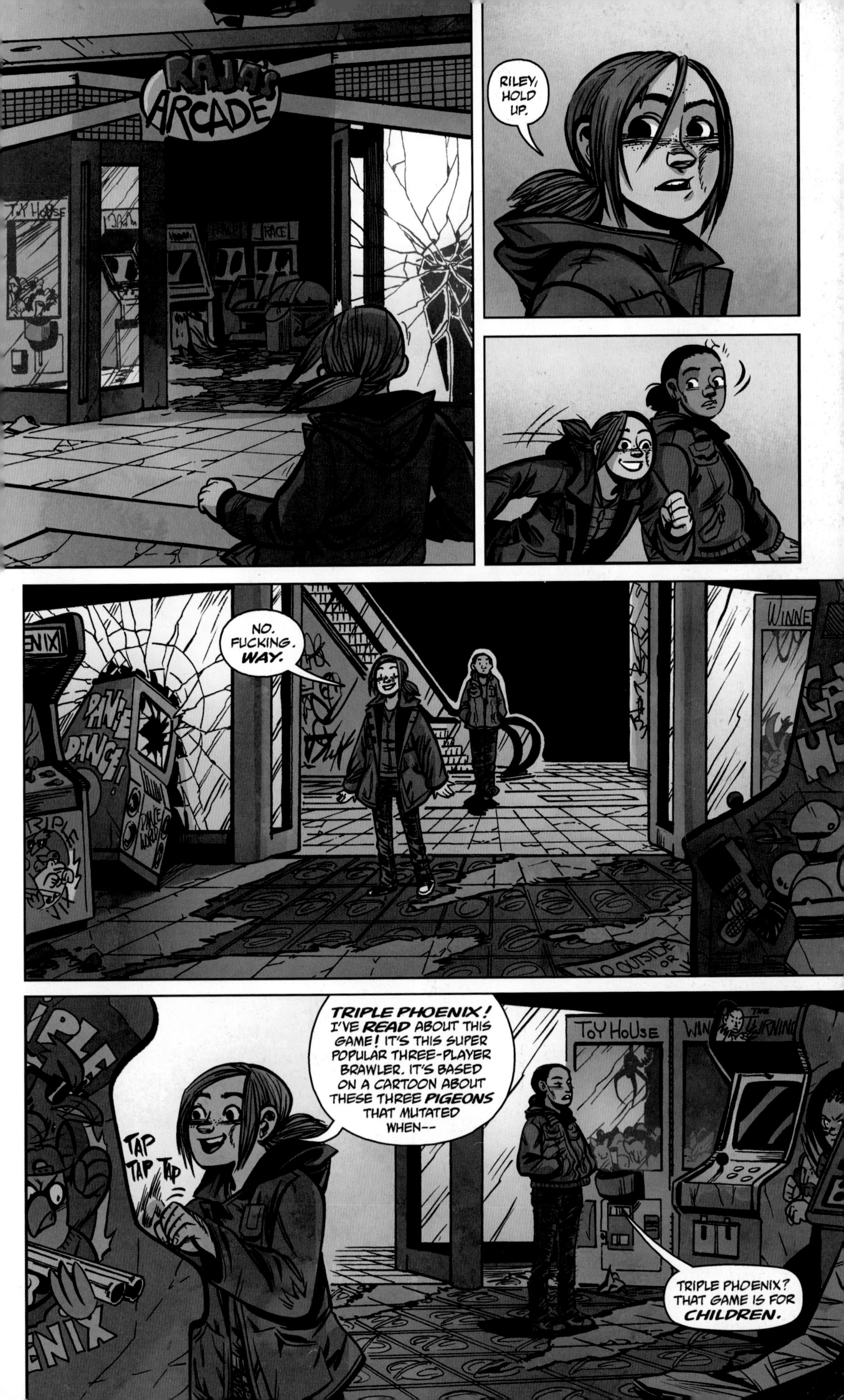
RAJA'S ARCADE
TOY HOUSE
RACE
RILEY, HOLD UP.
NO. FUCKING. WAY.
DANCE DANCE!
NO OUTSIDE
TRIPLE PHOENIX! I'VE READ ABOUT THIS GAME! IT'S THIS SUPER POPULAR THREE-PLAYER BRAWLER. IT'S BASED ON A CARTOON ABOUT THESE THREE PIGEONS THAT MUTATED WHEN--
TAP TAP TAP
TOY HOUSE
THE BURNING
TRIPLE PHOENIX? THAT GAME IS FOR CHILDREN.

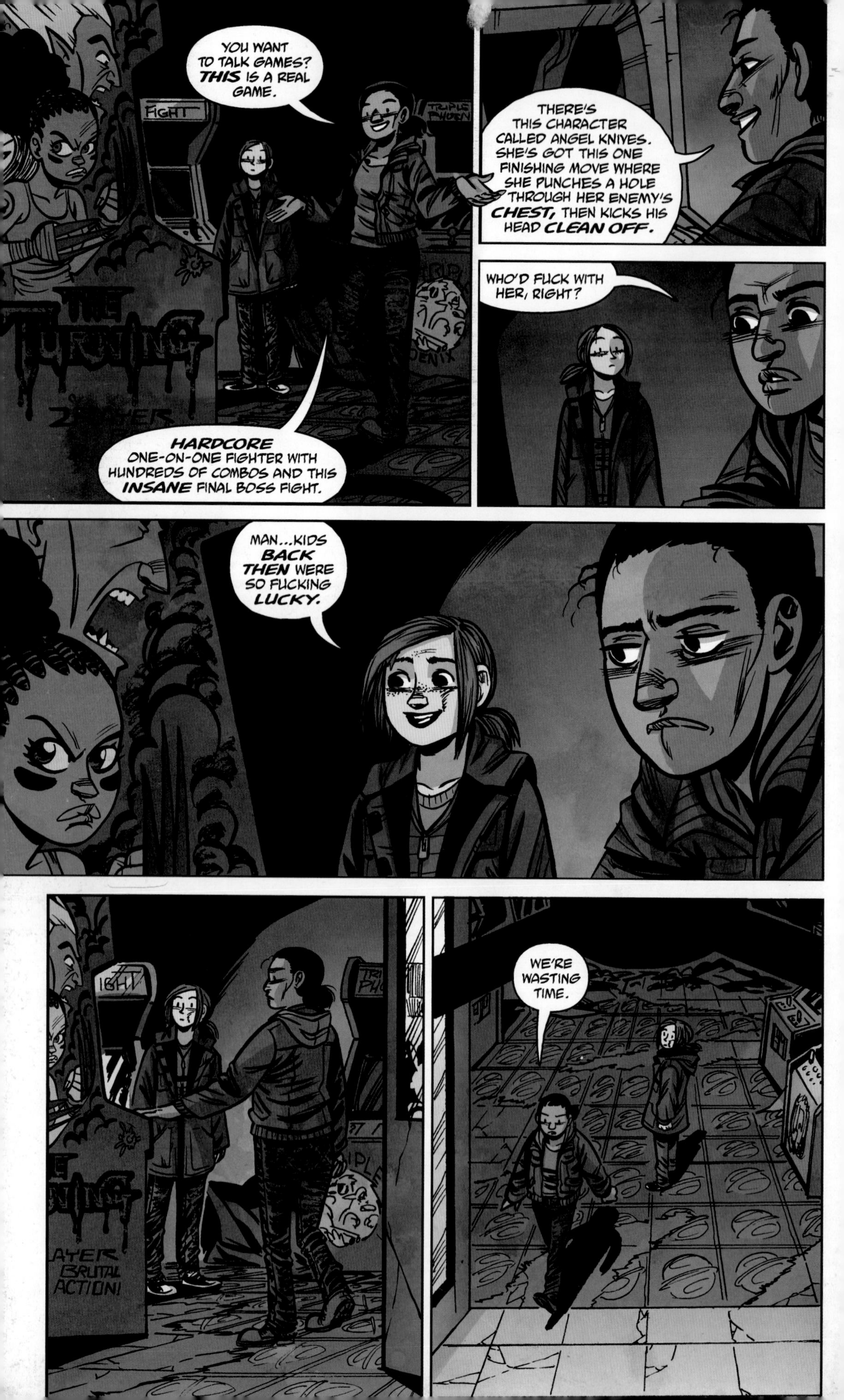
YOU WANT TO TALK GAMES? THIS IS A REAL GAME.
HARDCORE ONE-ON-ONE FIGHTER WITH HUNDREDS OF COMBOS AND THIS INSANE FINAL BOSS FIGHT.
THERE'S THIS CHARACTER CALLED ANGEL KNIVES. SHE'S GOT THIS ONE FINISHING MOVE WHERE SHE PUNCHES A HOLE THROUGH HER ENEMY'S CHEST, THEN KICKS HIS HEAD CLEAN OFF.
WHO'D FUCK WITH HER, RIGHT?
MAN...KIDS BACK THEN WERE SO FUCKING LUCKY.
WE'RE WASTING TIME.

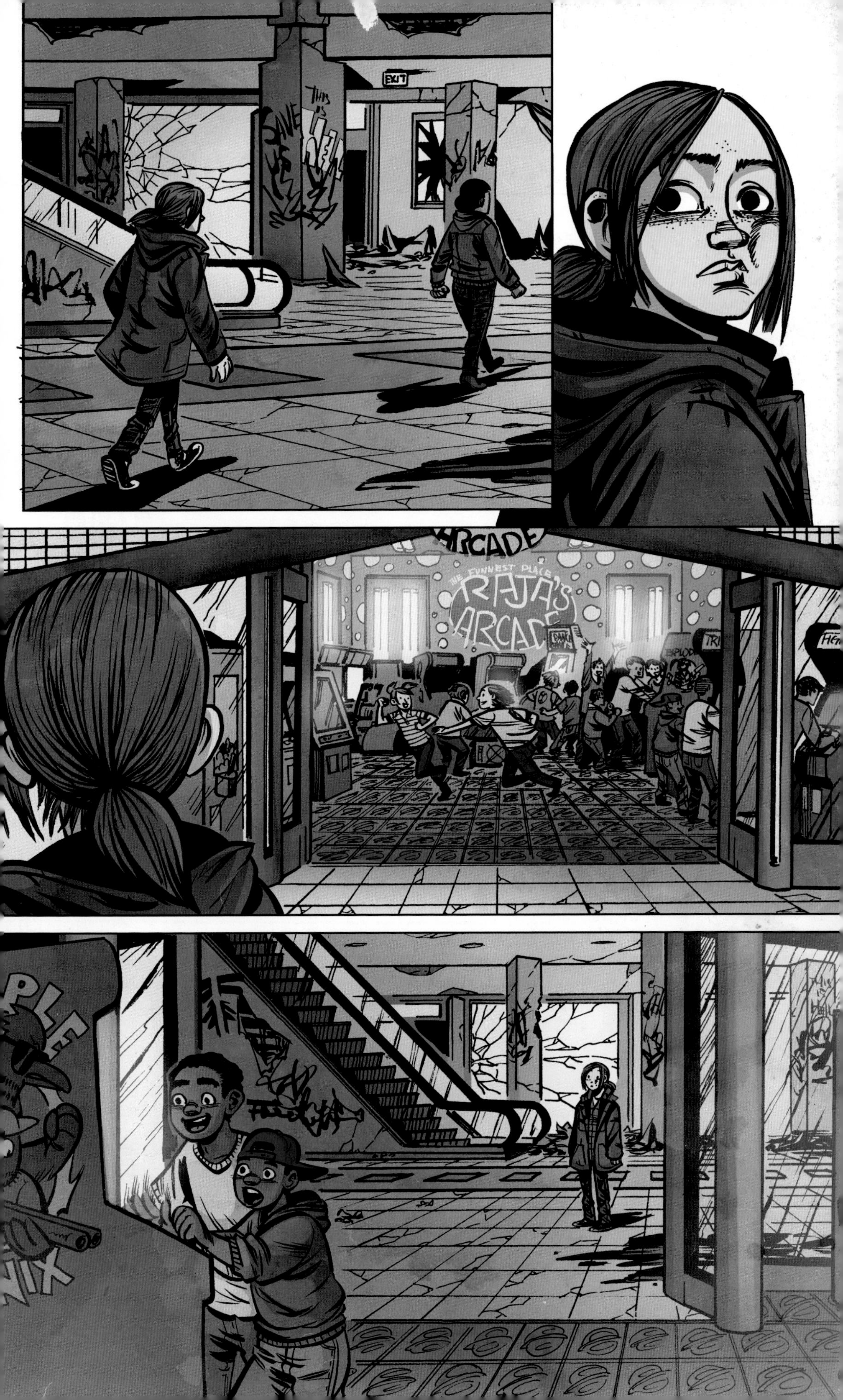

EXIT
ARCADE
THE FUNNEST PLACE
RAJA'S ARCADE

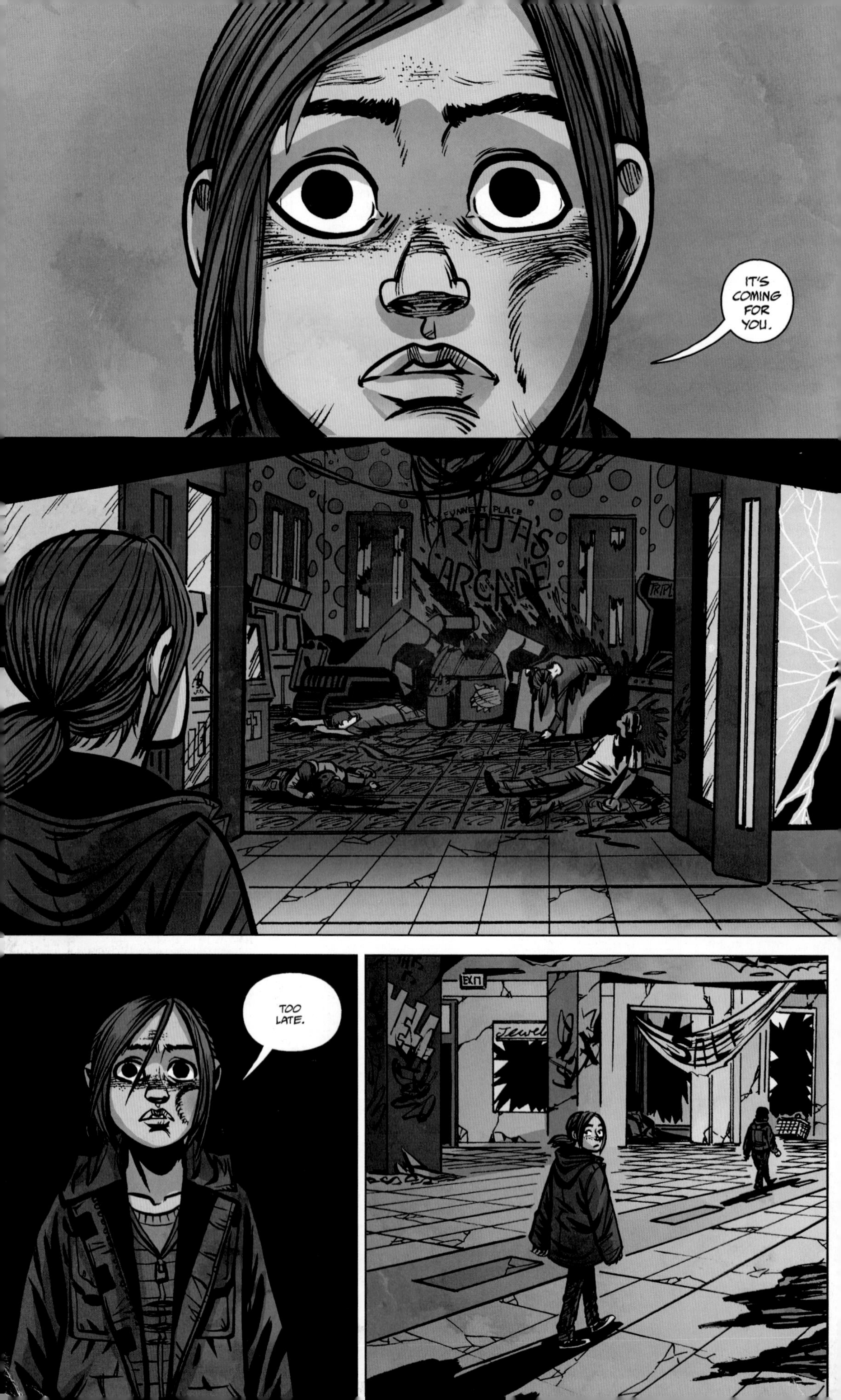
IT'S COMING FOR YOU.
FUNNEST PLACE
RAJA'S ARCADE
TOO LATE.
EXIT
SALE

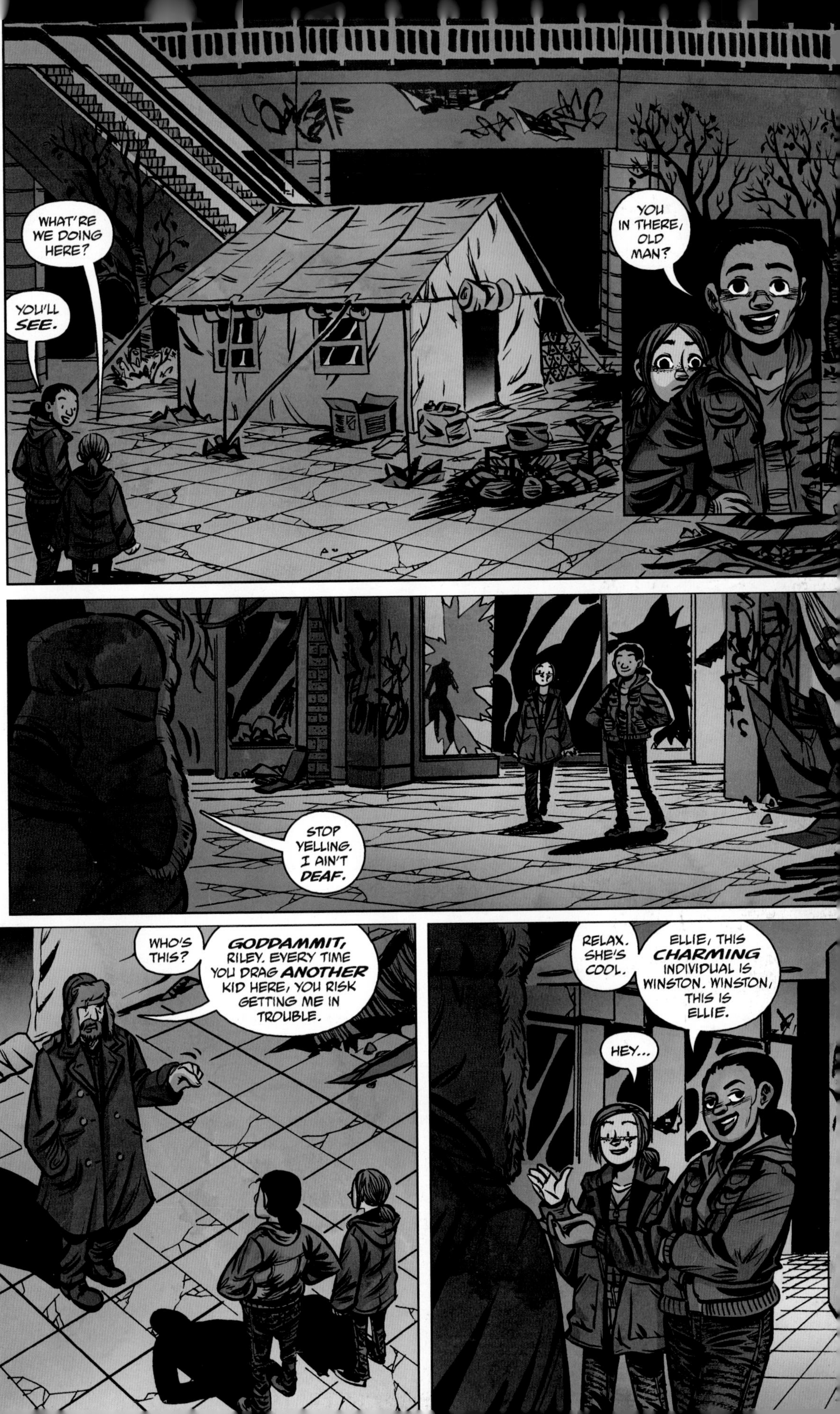
WHAT'RE WE DOING HERE?
YOU'LL **SEE.**
YOU IN THERE, OLD MAN?
STOP YELLING. I AIN'T **DEAF.**
WHO'S THIS?
GODDAMMIT, RILEY. EVERY TIME YOU DRAG **ANOTHER** KID HERE, YOU RISK GETTING ME IN TROUBLE.
RELAX. SHE'S COOL.
ELLIE, THIS **CHARMING** INDIVIDUAL IS WINSTON. WINSTON, THIS IS ELLIE.
HEY...

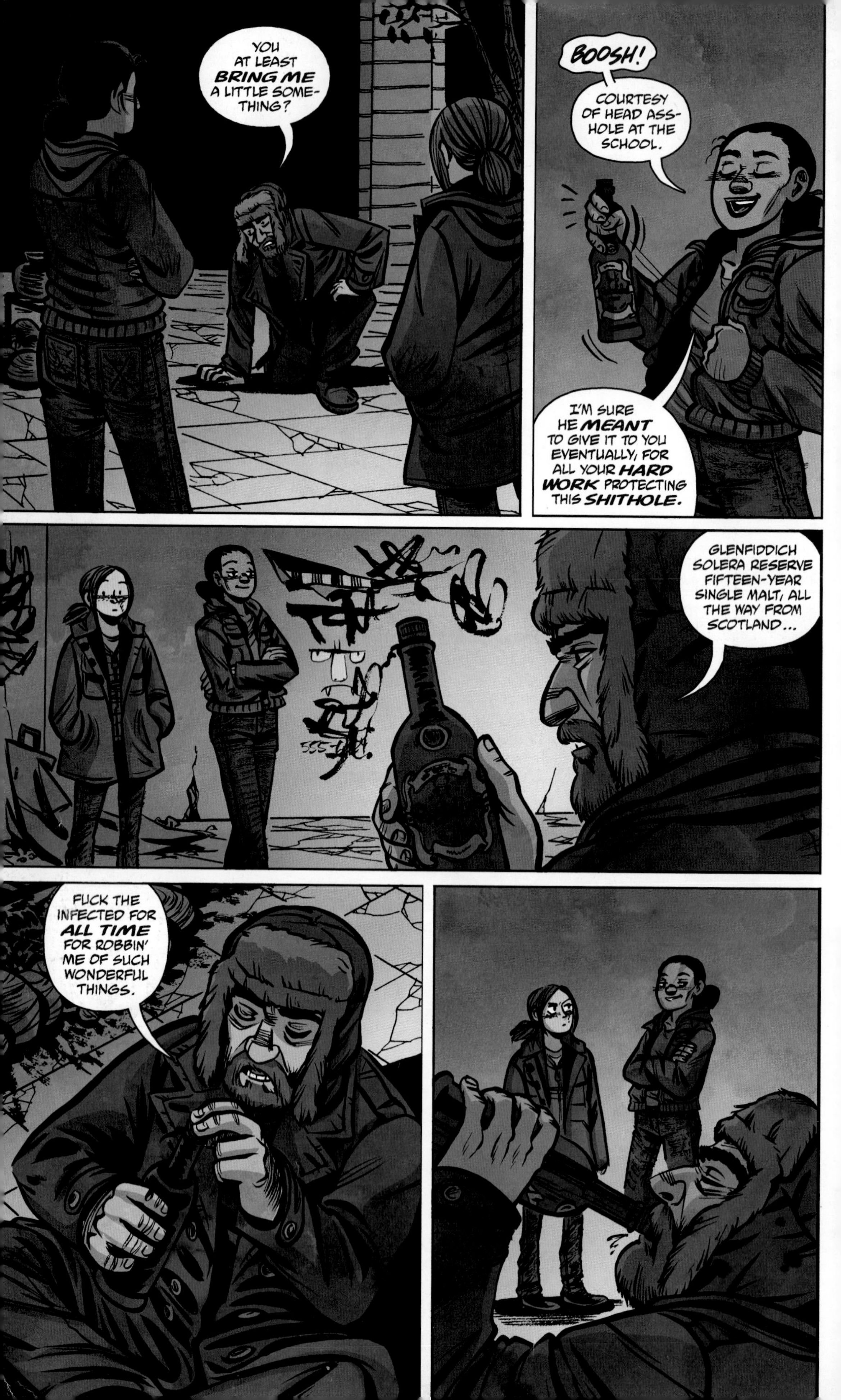
YOU AT LEAST BRING ME A LITTLE SOMETHING?
BOOSH!
COURTESY OF HEAD ASSHOLE AT THE SCHOOL.
I'M SURE HE MEANT TO GIVE IT TO YOU EVENTUALLY, FOR ALL YOUR HARD WORK PROTECTING THIS SHITHOLE.
GLENFIDDICH SOLERA RESERVE FIFTEEN-YEAR SINGLE MALT, ALL THE WAY FROM SCOTLAND...
FUCK THE INFECTED FOR ALL TIME FOR ROBBIN' ME OF SUCH WONDERFUL THINGS.

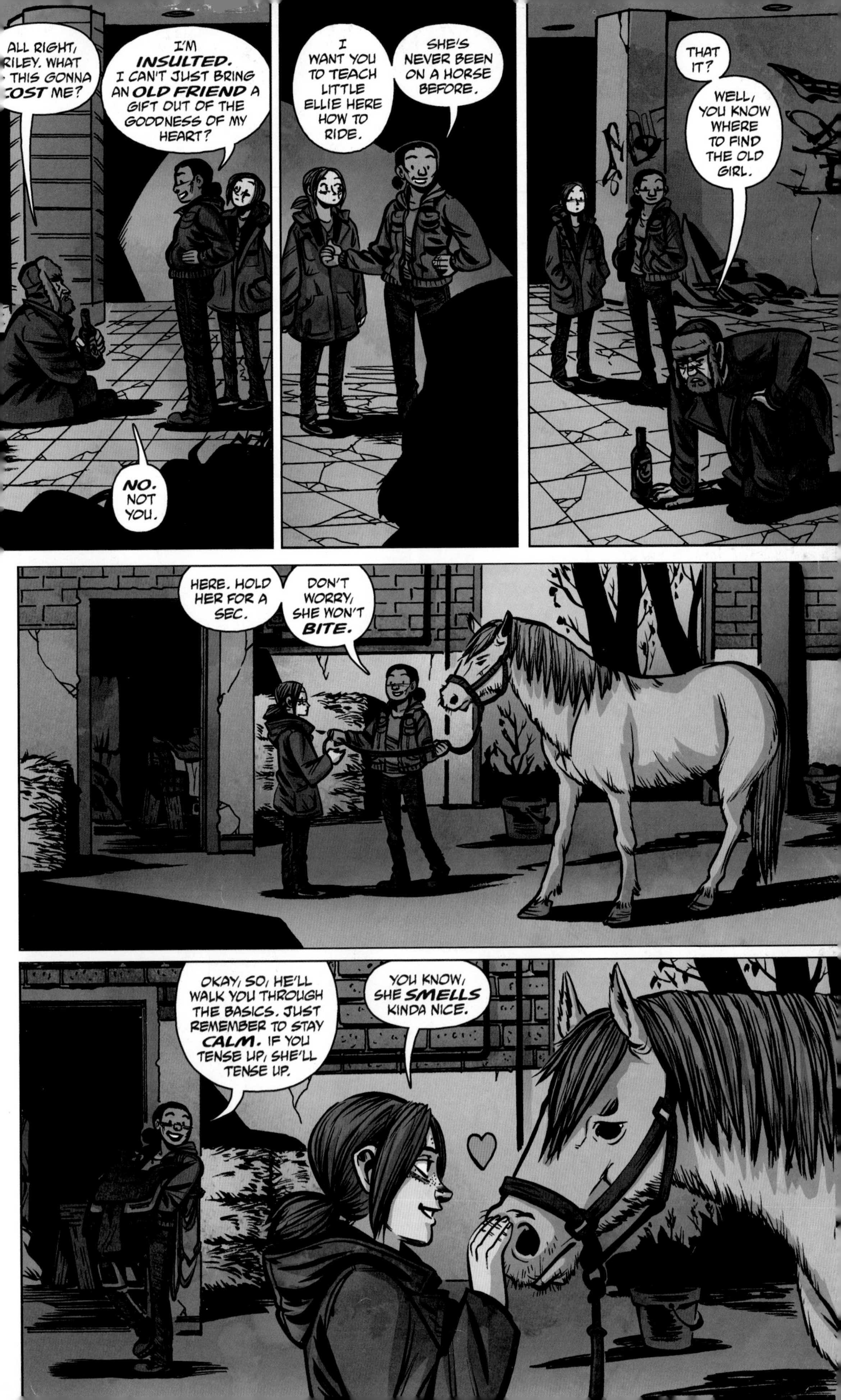

ALL RIGHT, RILEY. WHAT'S THIS GONNA COST ME?
I'M INSULTED. I CAN'T JUST BRING AN OLD FRIEND A GIFT OUT OF THE GOODNESS OF MY HEART?
NO. NOT YOU.
I WANT YOU TO TEACH LITTLE ELLIE HERE HOW TO RIDE.
SHE'S NEVER BEEN ON A HORSE BEFORE.
THAT IT?
WELL, YOU KNOW WHERE TO FIND THE OLD GIRL.
HERE. HOLD HER FOR A SEC.
DON'T WORRY, SHE WON'T BITE.
OKAY, SO, HE'LL WALK YOU THROUGH THE BASICS. JUST REMEMBER TO STAY CALM. IF YOU TENSE UP, SHE'LL TENSE UP.
YOU KNOW, SHE SMELLS KINDA NICE.

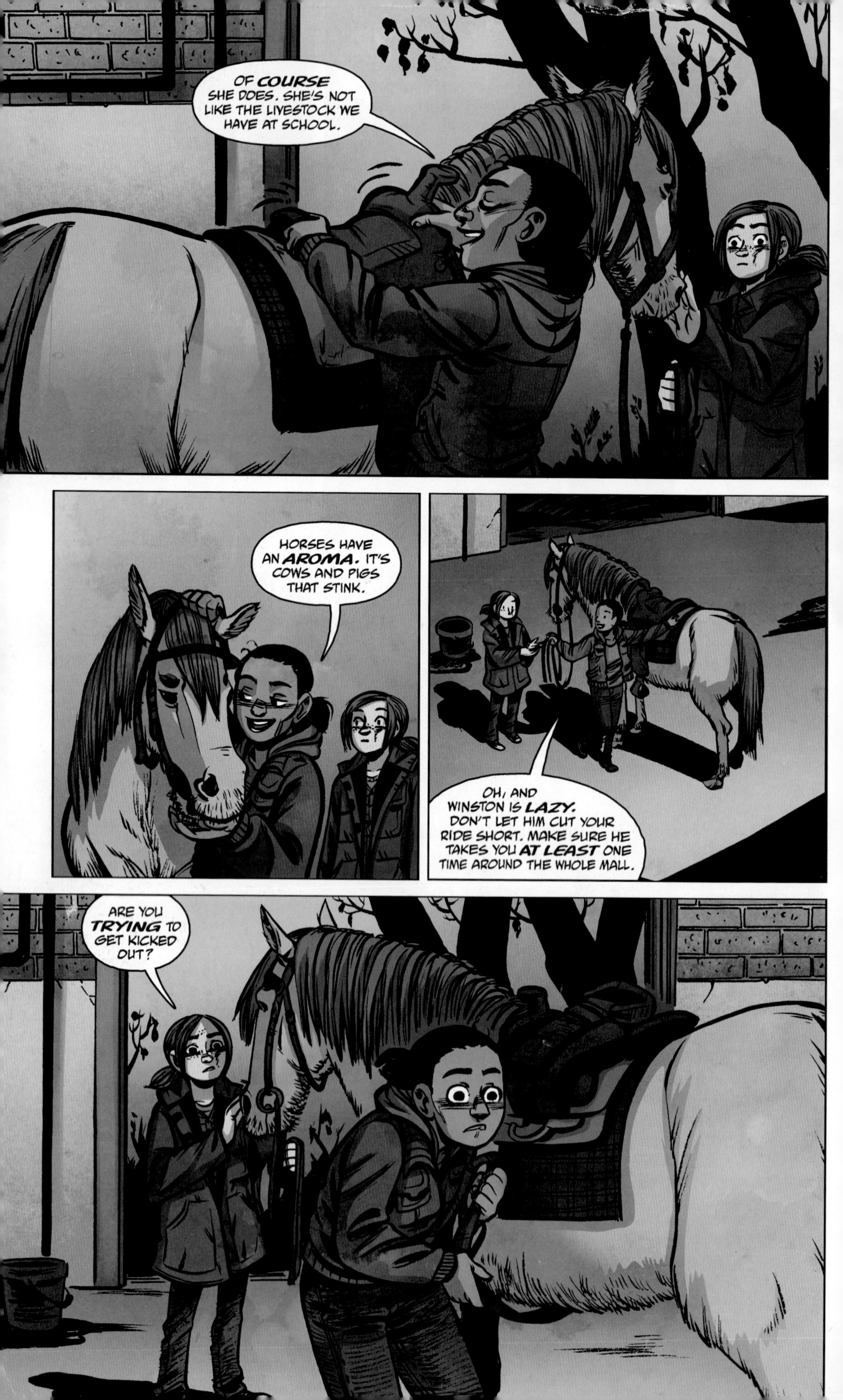
OF COURSE SHE DOES. SHE'S NOT LIKE THE LIVESTOCK WE HAVE AT SCHOOL.
HORSES HAVE AN AROMA. IT'S COWS AND PIGS THAT STINK.
OH, AND WINSTON IS LAZY. DON'T LET HIM CUT YOUR RIDE SHORT. MAKE SURE HE TAKES YOU AT LEAST ONE TIME AROUND THE WHOLE MALL.
ARE YOU TRYING TO GET KICKED OUT?

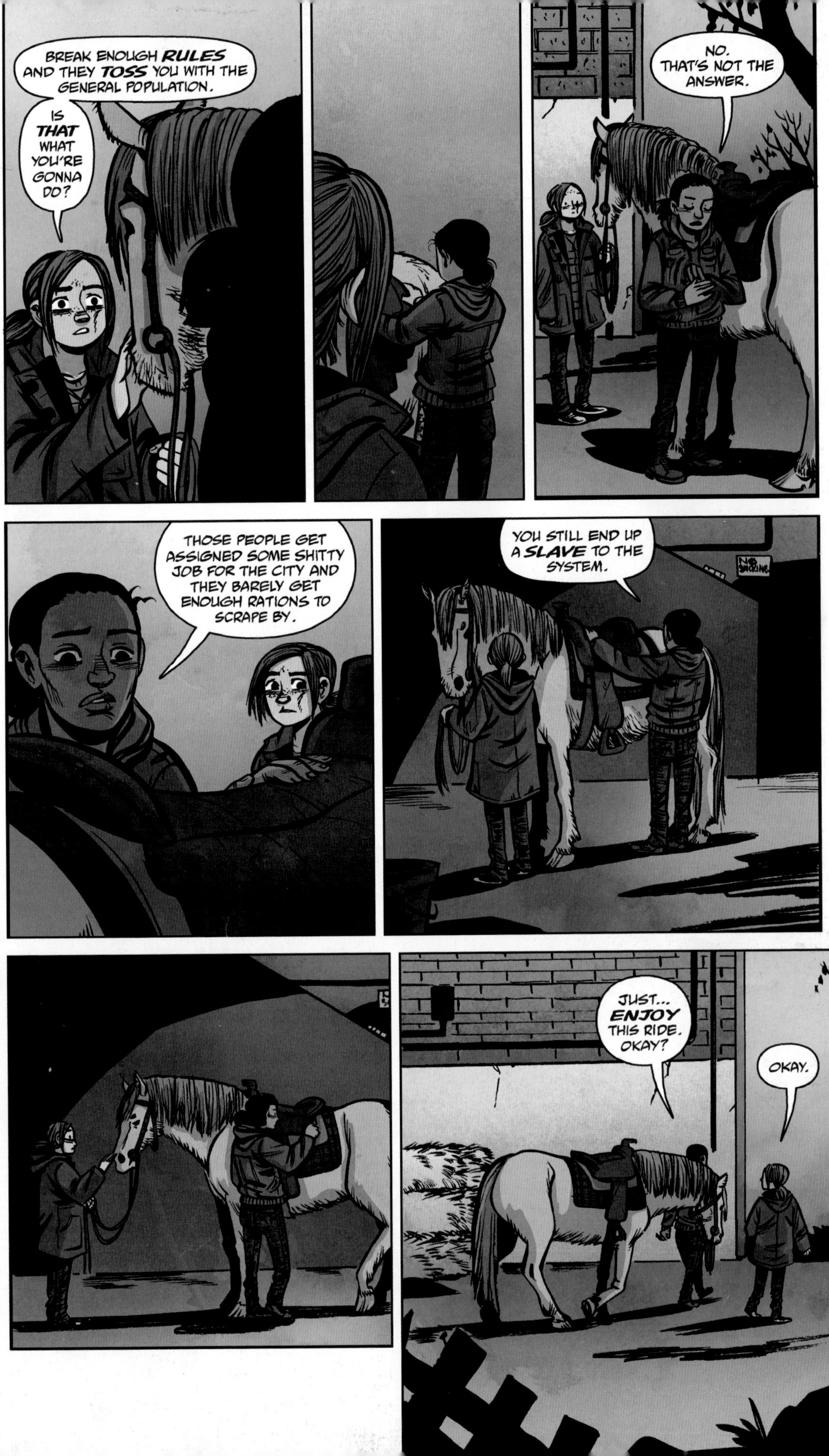
BREAK ENOUGH RULES AND THEY TOSS YOU WITH THE GENERAL POPULATION.
IS THAT WHAT YOU'RE GONNA DO?
NO. THAT'S NOT THE ANSWER.
THOSE PEOPLE GET ASSIGNED SOME SHITTY JOB FOR THE CITY AND THEY BARELY GET ENOUGH RATIONS TO SCRAPE BY.
YOU STILL END UP A SLAVE TO THE SYSTEM.
NO SMOKING
JUST... ENJOY THIS RIDE. OKAY?
OKAY.

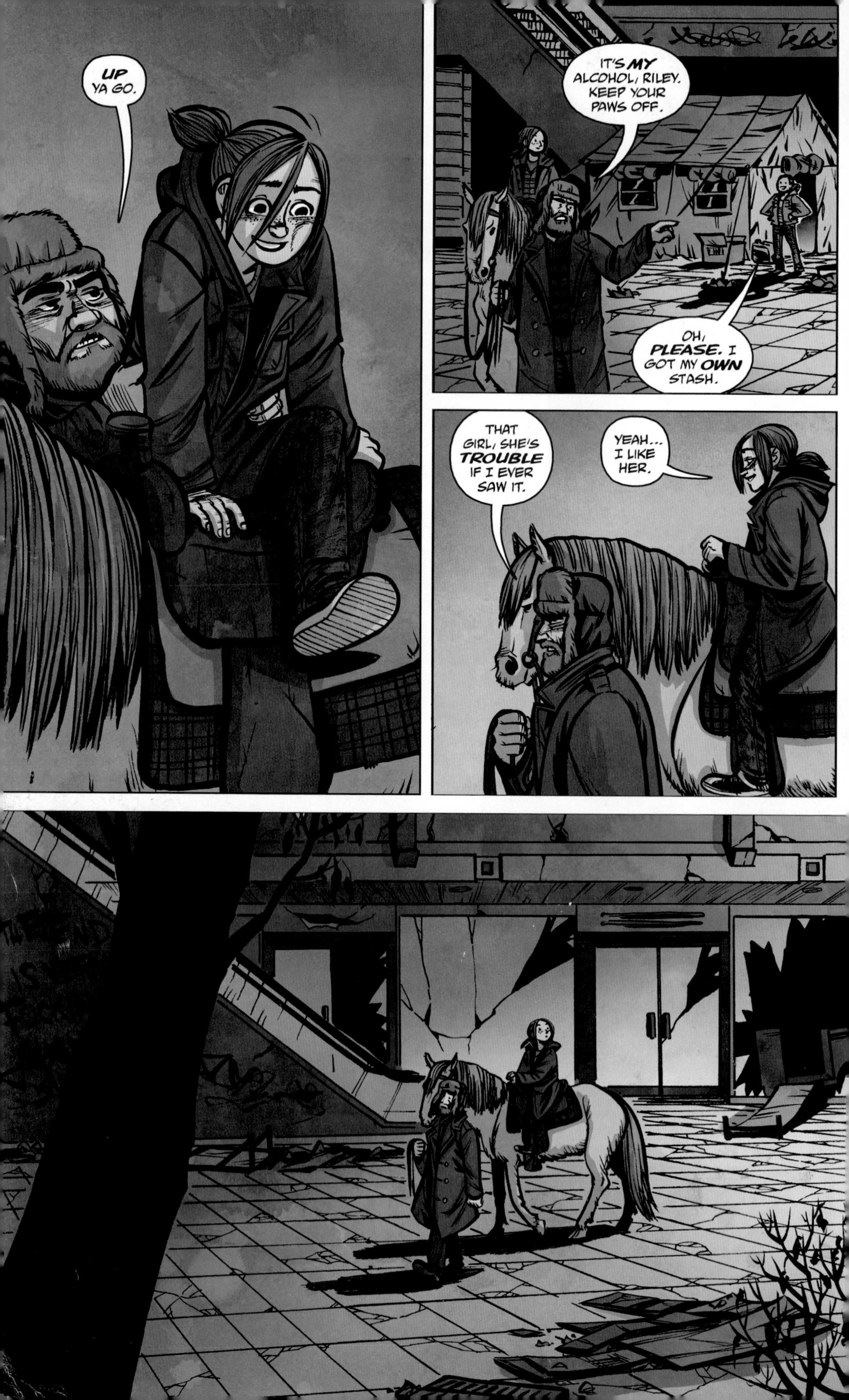
UP YA GO.
IT'S MY ALCOHOL, RILEY. KEEP YOUR PAWS OFF.
OH, PLEASE. I GOT MY OWN STASH.
THAT GIRL, SHE'S TROUBLE IF I EVER SAW IT.
YEAH... I LIKE HER.

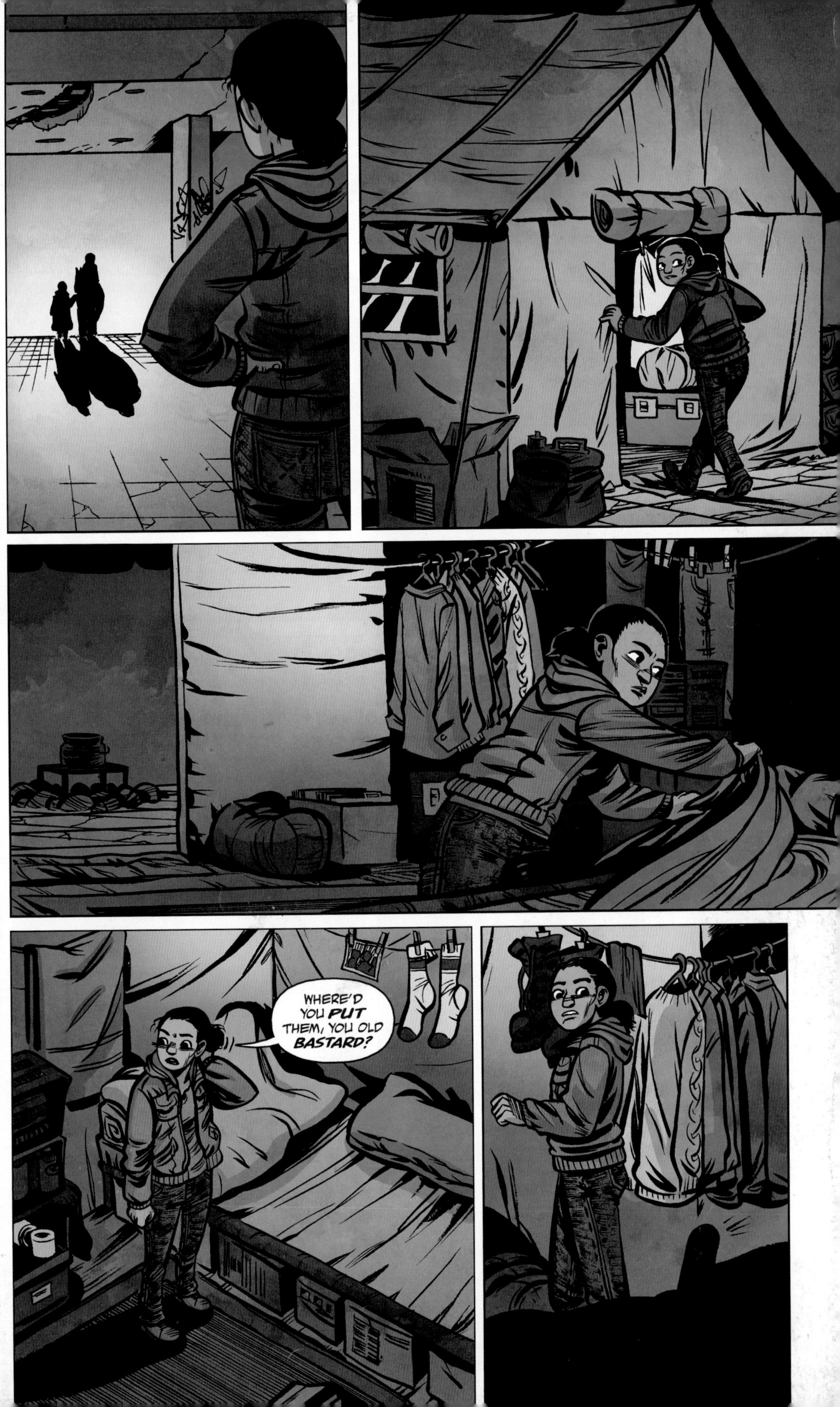
WHERE'D YOU PUT THEM, YOU OLD BASTARD?

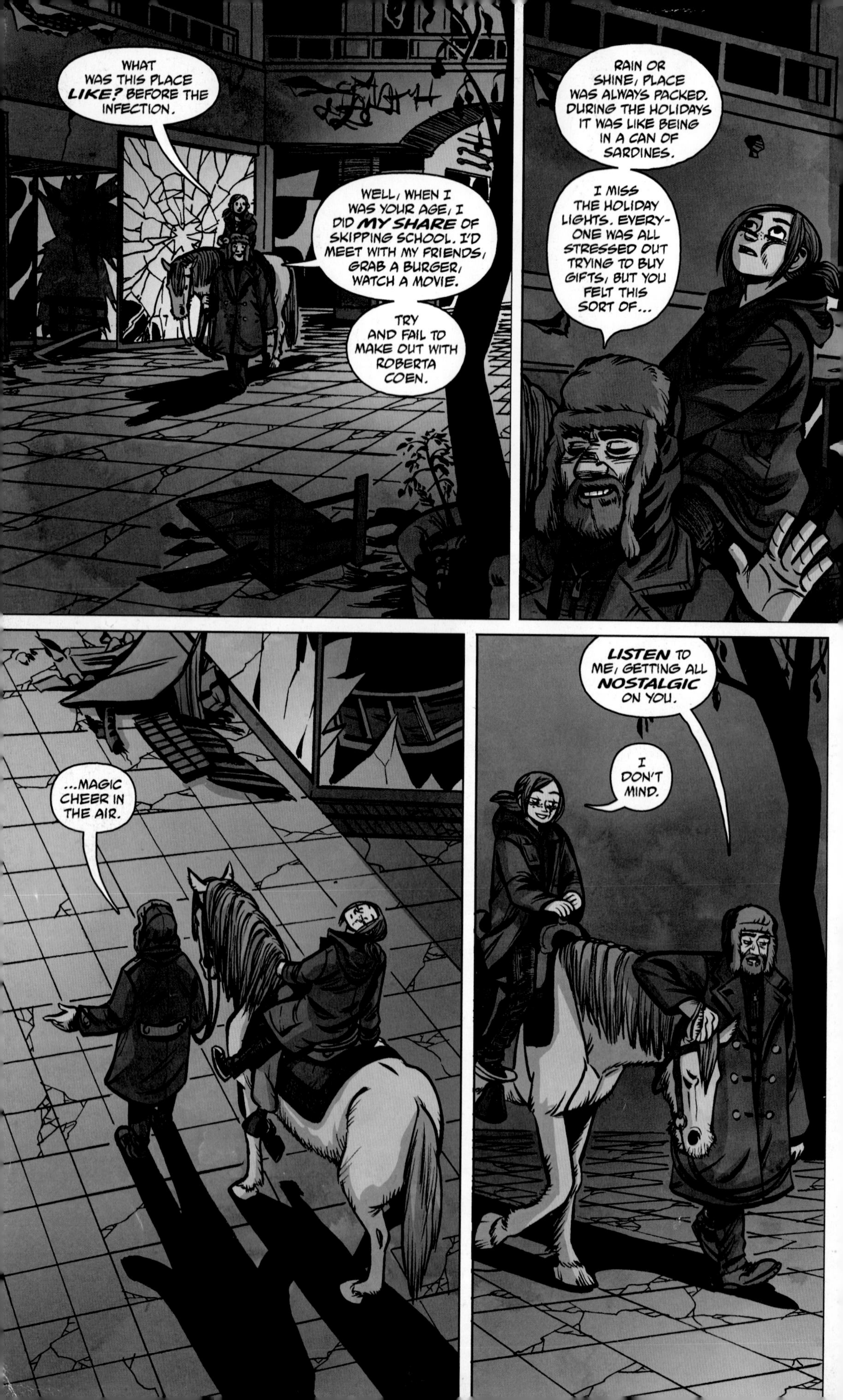
WHAT WAS THIS PLACE LIKE? BEFORE THE INFECTION.
WELL, WHEN I WAS YOUR AGE, I DID MY SHARE OF SKIPPING SCHOOL. I'D MEET WITH MY FRIENDS, GRAB A BURGER, WATCH A MOVIE.
TRY AND FAIL TO MAKE OUT WITH ROBERTA COEN.
RAIN OR SHINE, PLACE WAS ALWAYS PACKED. DURING THE HOLIDAYS IT WAS LIKE BEING IN A CAN OF SARDINES.
I MISS THE HOLIDAY LIGHTS. EVERY-ONE WAS ALL STRESSED OUT TRYING TO BUY GIFTS, BUT YOU FELT THIS SORT OF...
...MAGIC CHEER IN THE AIR.
LISTEN TO ME, GETTING ALL NOSTALGIC ON YOU.
I DON'T MIND.

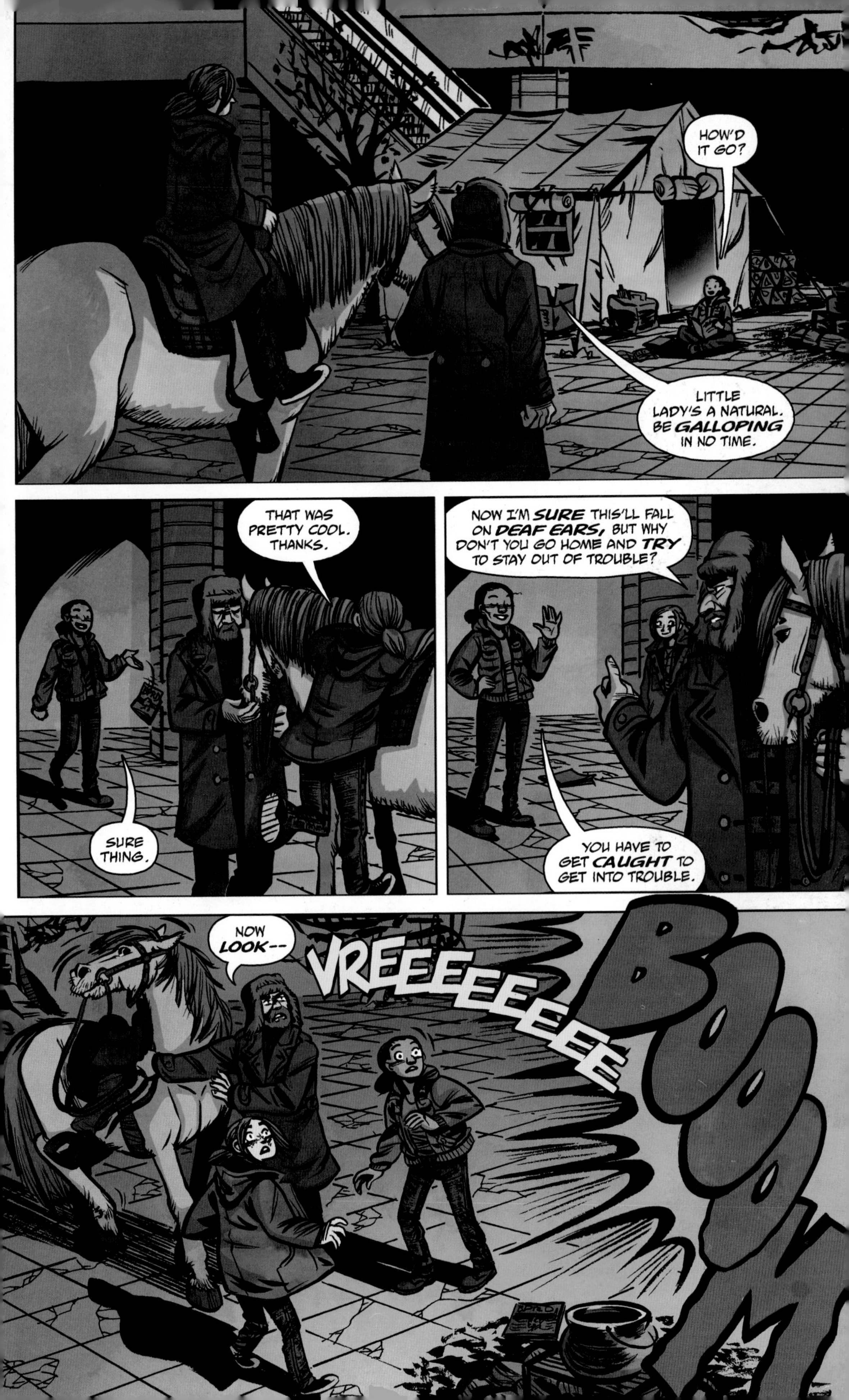
HOW'D IT GO?
LITTLE LADY'S A NATURAL. BE GALLOPING IN NO TIME.
THAT WAS PRETTY COOL. THANKS.
SURE THING.
NOW I'M SURE THIS'LL FALL ON DEAF EARS, BUT WHY DON'T YOU GO HOME AND TRY TO STAY OUT OF TROUBLE?
YOU HAVE TO GET CAUGHT TO GET INTO TROUBLE.
NOW LOOK--
VREEEEEEEEE
BOOOOM

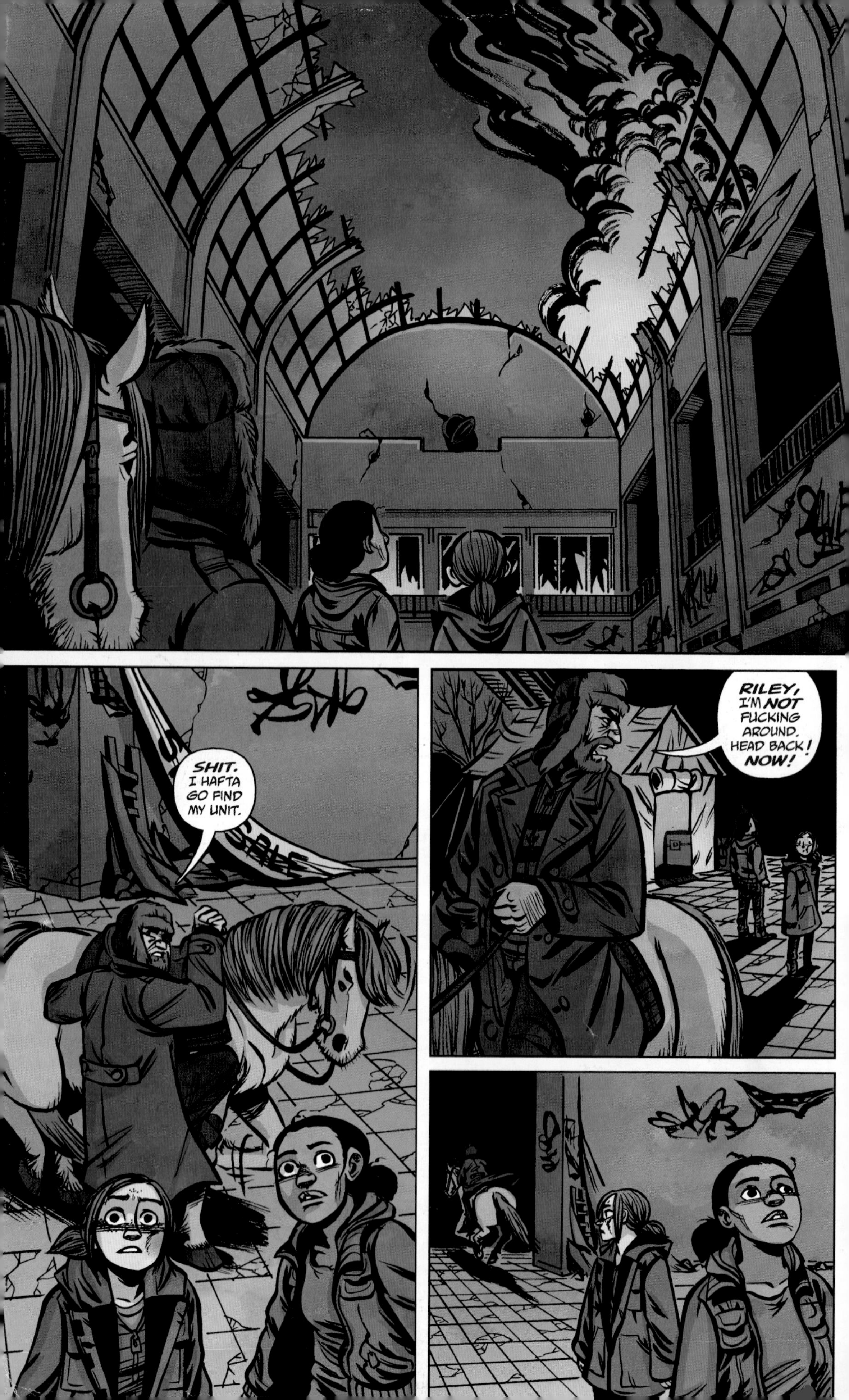
SHIT. I HAFTA GO FIND MY UNIT.
RILEY, I'M NOT FUCKING AROUND. HEAD BACK! NOW!

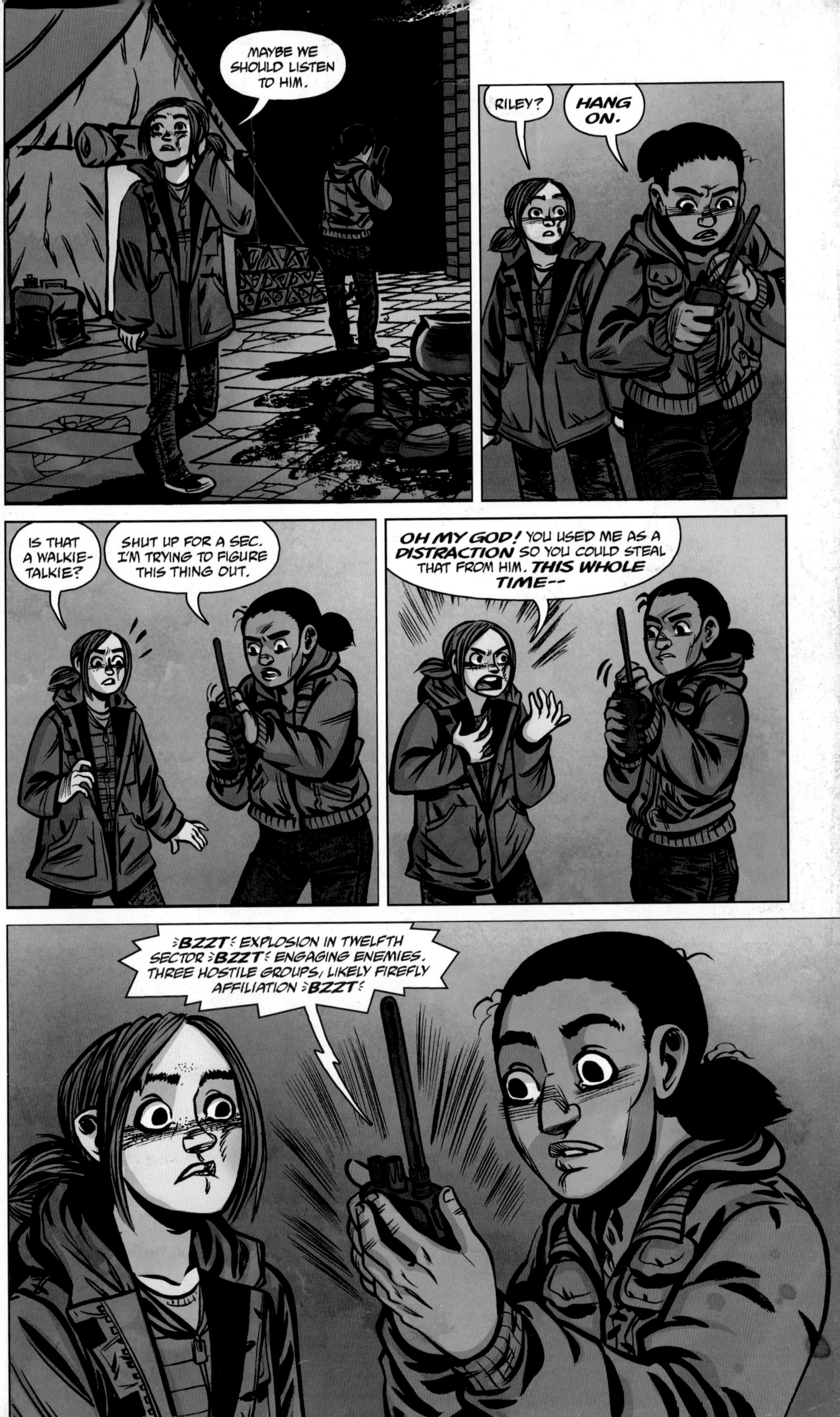
MAYBE WE SHOULD LISTEN TO HIM.
RILEY?
HANG ON.
IS THAT A WALKIE-TALKIE?
SHUT UP FOR A SEC. I'M TRYING TO FIGURE THIS THING OUT.
OH MY GOD! YOU USED ME AS A DISTRACTION SO YOU COULD STEAL THAT FROM HIM. THIS WHOLE TIME--
BZZT EXPLOSION IN TWELFTH SECTOR BZZT ENGAGING ENEMIES. THREE HOSTILE GROUPS, LIKELY FIREFLY AFFILIATION BZZT

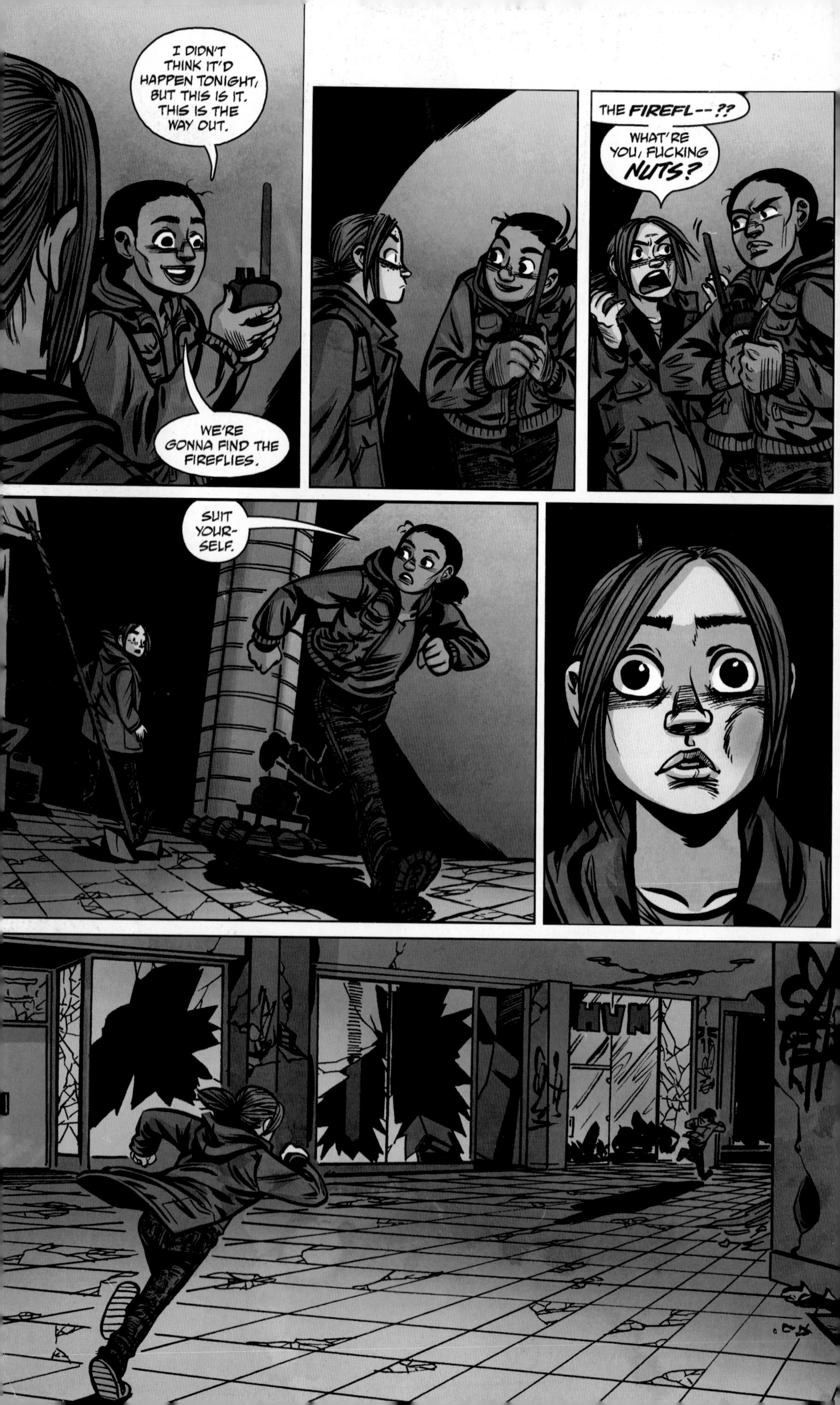
I DIDN'T THINK IT'D HAPPEN TONIGHT, BUT THIS IS IT. THIS IS THE WAY OUT.
WE'RE GONNA FIND THE FIREFLIES.
THE FIREFL--??
WHAT'RE YOU, FUCKING NUTS?
SUIT YOUR-SELF.
HVM

CHAPTER THREE

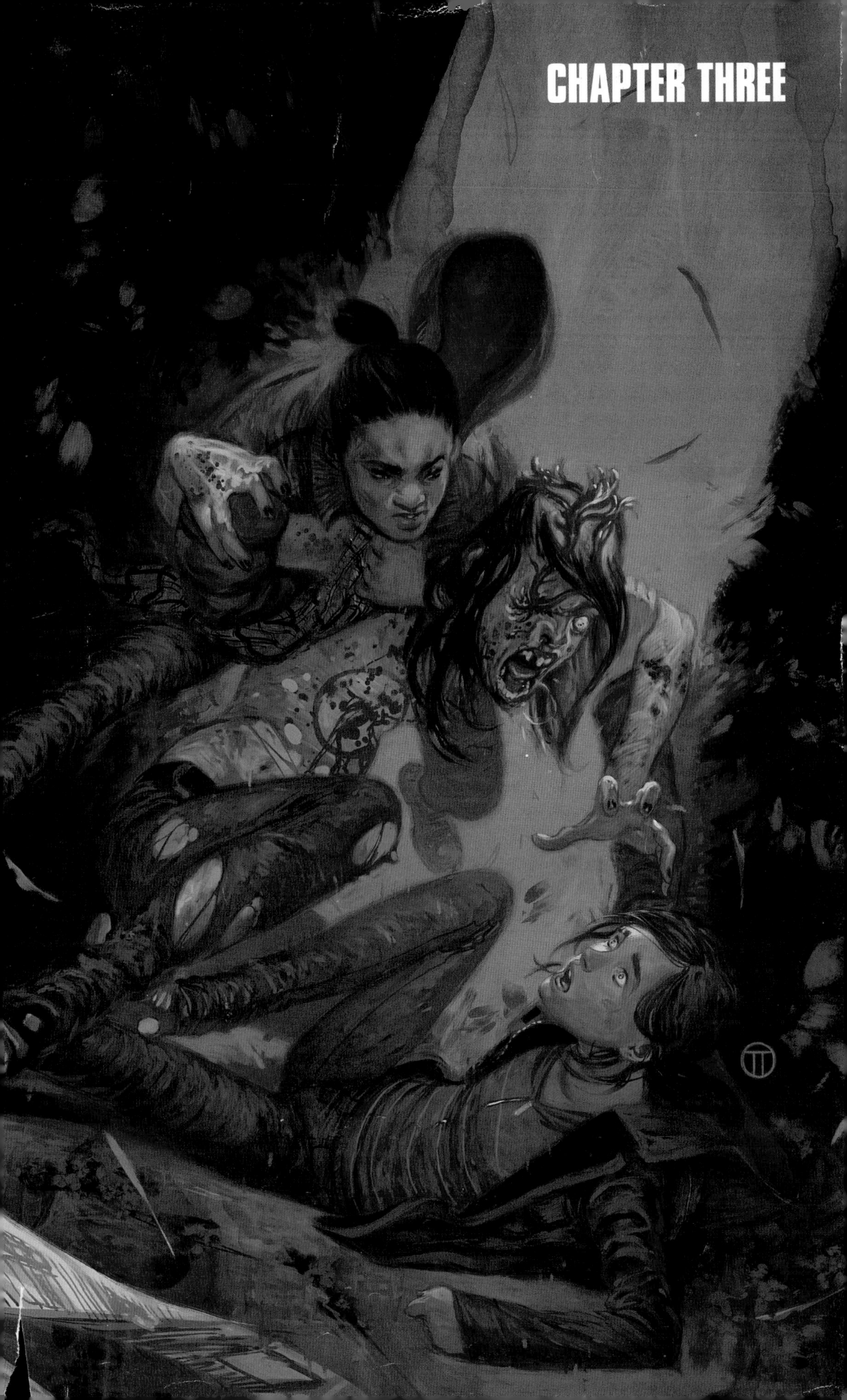

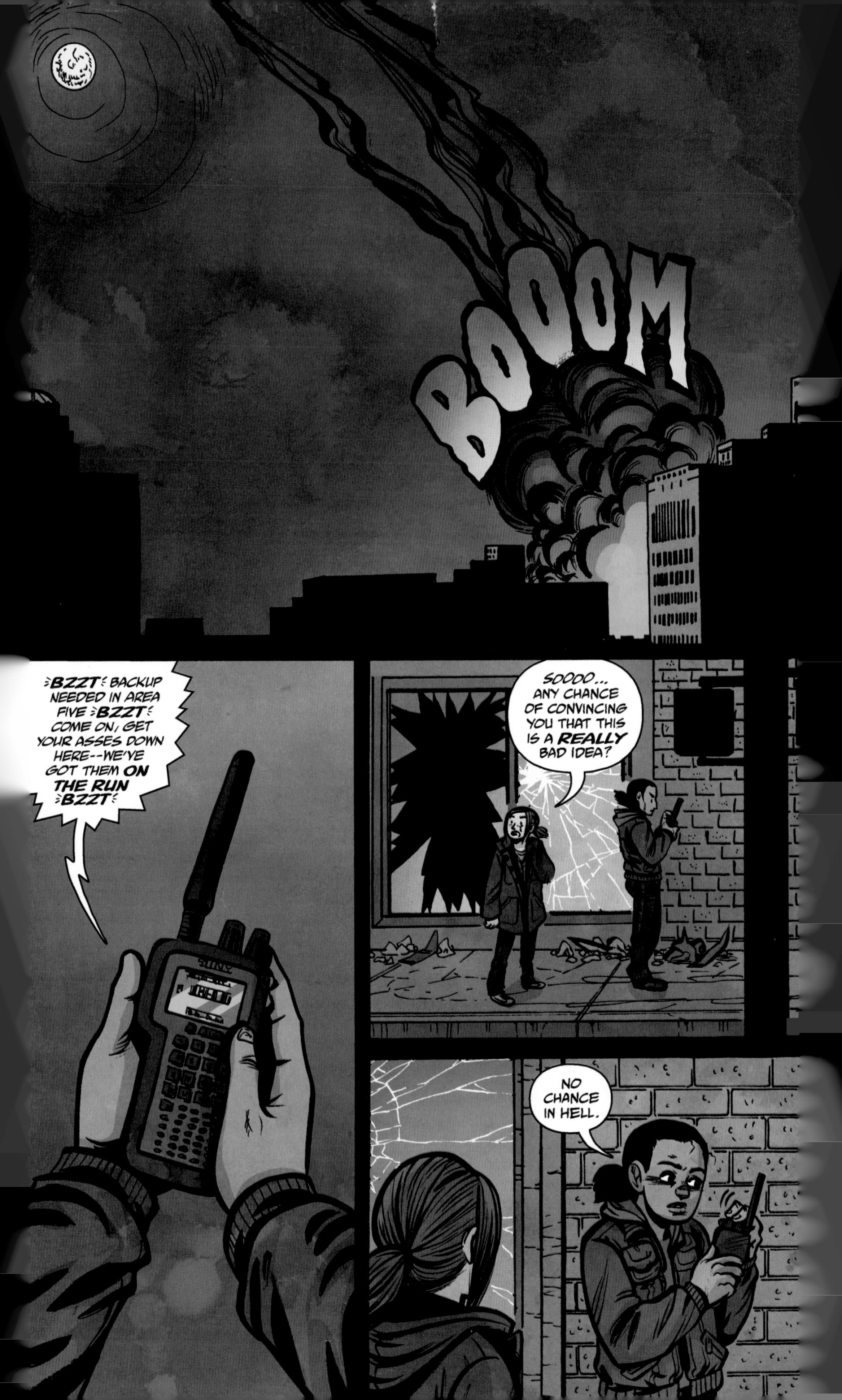
BOOOM
BZZT BACKUP NEEDED IN AREA FIVE BZZT COME ON, GET YOUR ASSES DOWN HERE--WE'VE GOT THEM ON THE RUN BZZT
SOOOO... ANY CHANCE OF CONVINCING YOU THAT THIS IS A REALLY BAD IDEA?
NO CHANCE IN HELL.

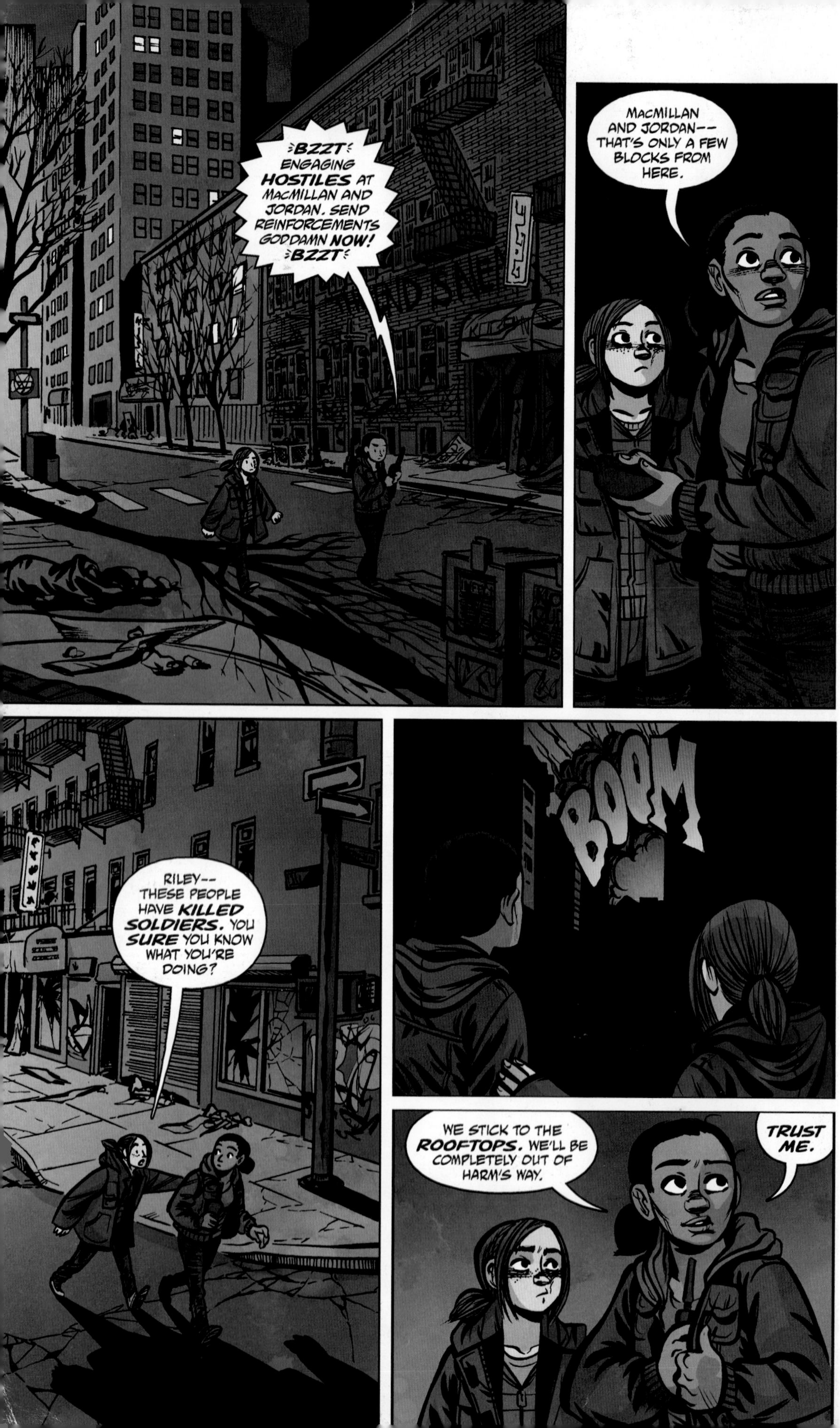
BZZT ENGAGING HOSTILES AT MACMILLAN AND JORDAN. SEND REINFORCEMENTS GODDAMN NOW! BZZT
MACMILLAN AND JORDAN-- THAT'S ONLY A FEW BLOCKS FROM HERE.
RILEY-- THESE PEOPLE HAVE KILLED SOLDIERS. YOU SURE YOU KNOW WHAT YOU'RE DOING?
BOOM
WE STICK TO THE ROOFTOPS. WE'LL BE COMPLETELY OUT OF HARM'S WAY.
TRUST ME.

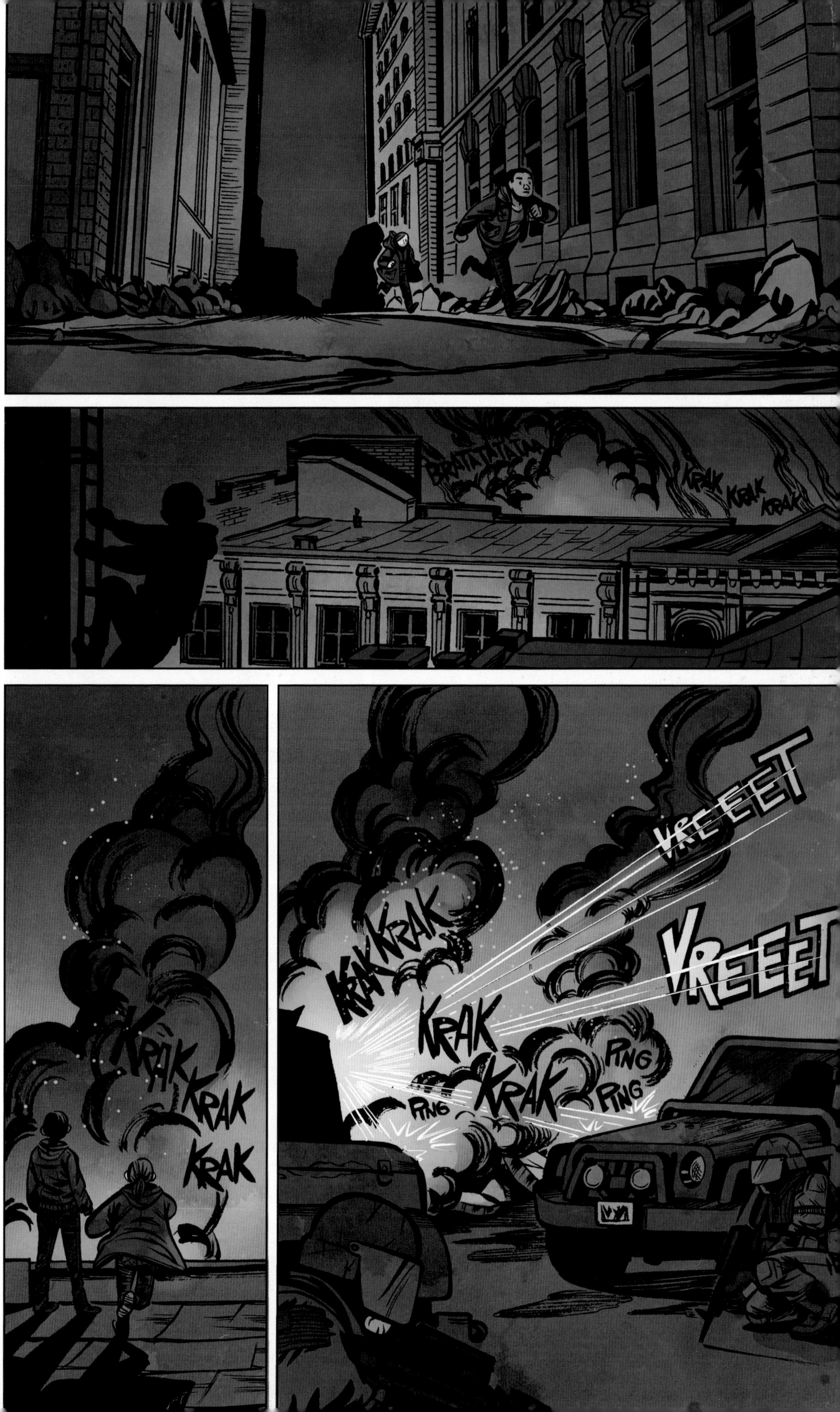
BRATATATATAM
KRAK KRAK KRAK
KRAK KRAK
KRAK
VREEET
VREEET
KRAK KRAK
KRAK
KRAK
PING
PING
PING

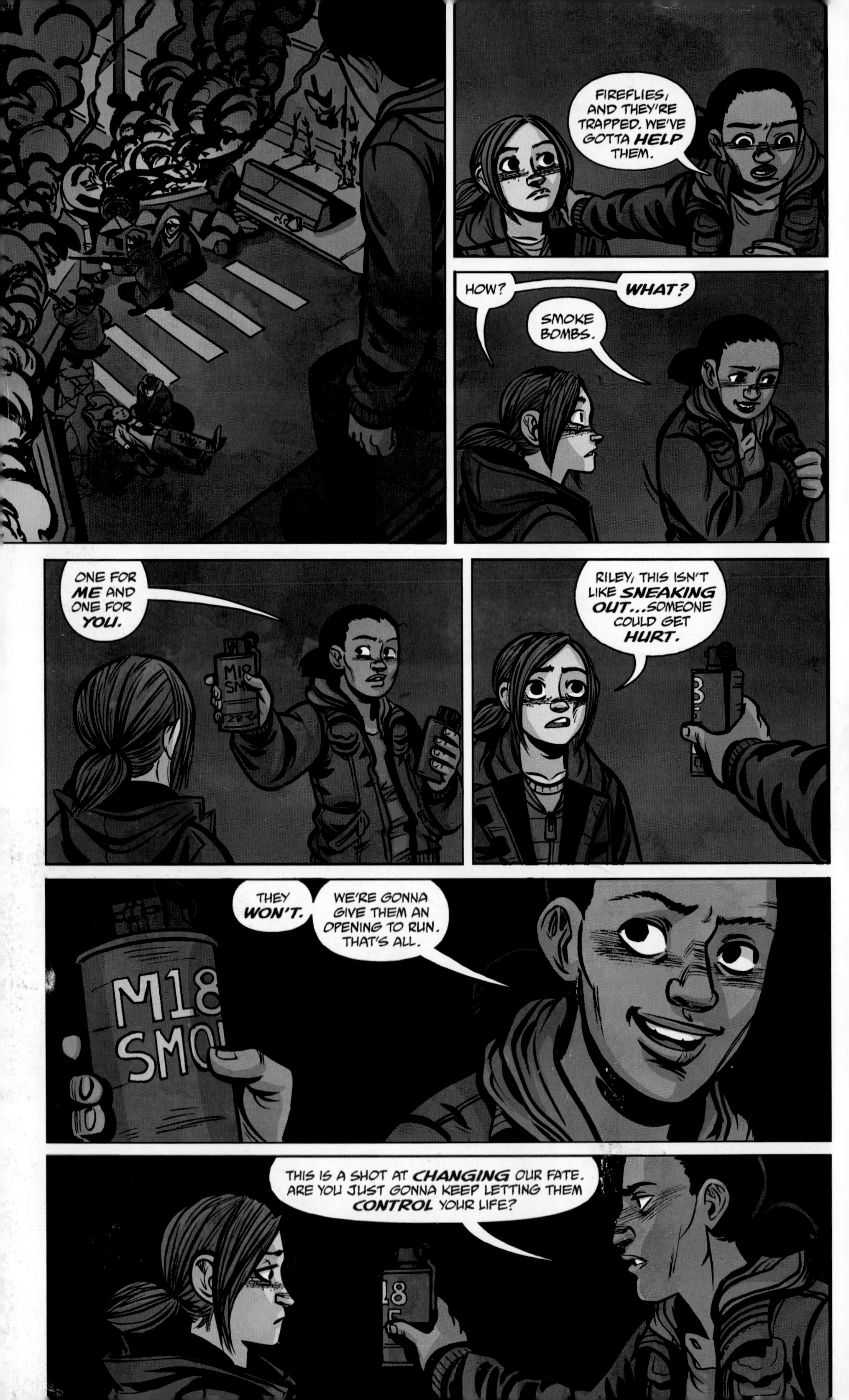
FIREFLIES, AND THEY'RE TRAPPED. WE'VE GOTTA HELP THEM.
HOW?
WHAT?
SMOKE BOMBS.
ONE FOR ME AND ONE FOR YOU.
RILEY, THIS ISN'T LIKE SNEAKING OUT...SOMEONE COULD GET HURT.
THEY WON'T.
WE'RE GONNA GIVE THEM AN OPENING TO RUN. THAT'S ALL.
M18 SMO
THIS IS A SHOT AT CHANGING OUR FATE. ARE YOU JUST GONNA KEEP LETTING THEM CONTROL YOUR LIFE?

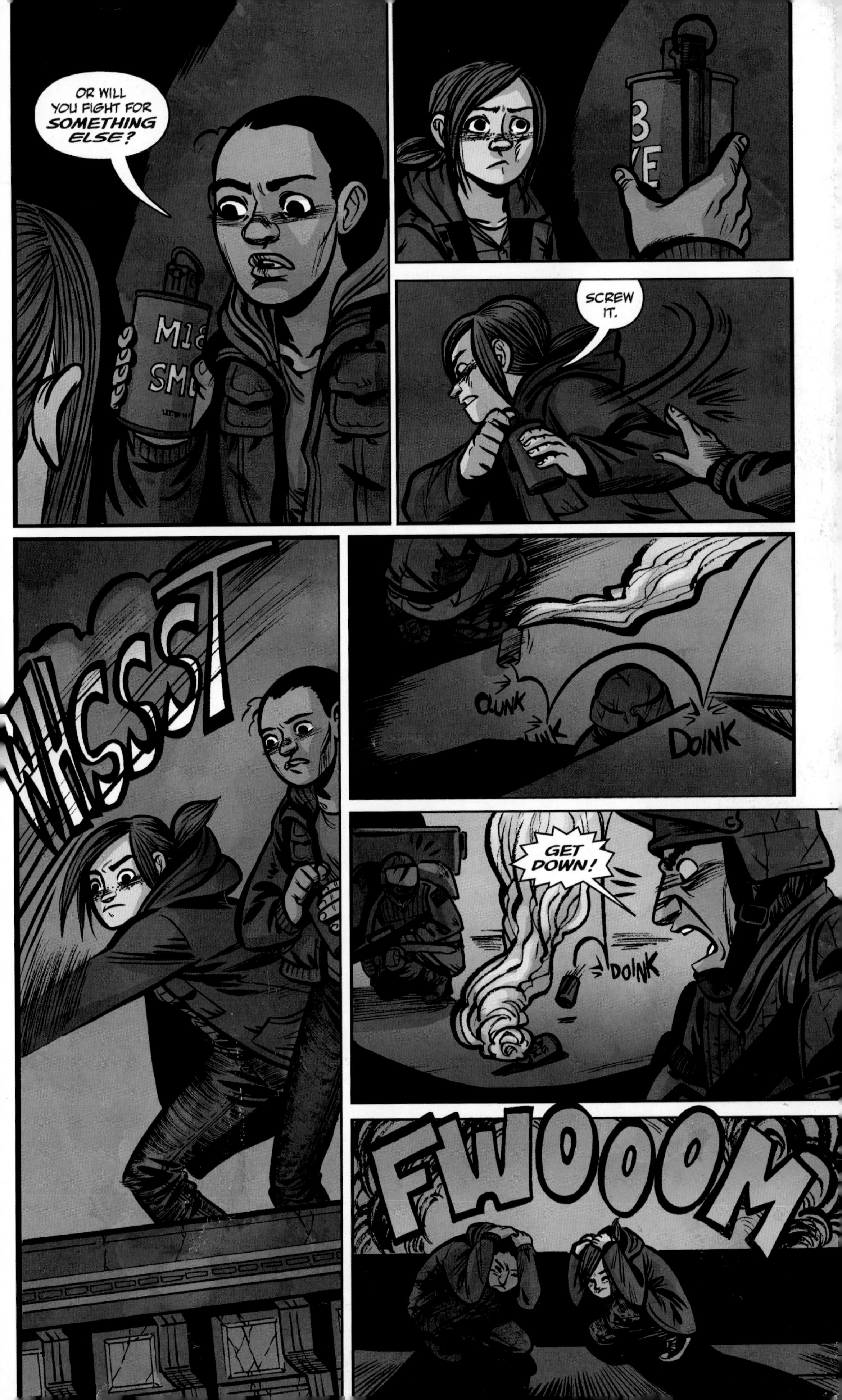

OR WILL YOU FIGHT FOR SOMETHING ELSE?
M18 SM
SCREW IT.
WHSSST
CLUNK
DOINK
GET DOWN!
DOINK
FWOOOM

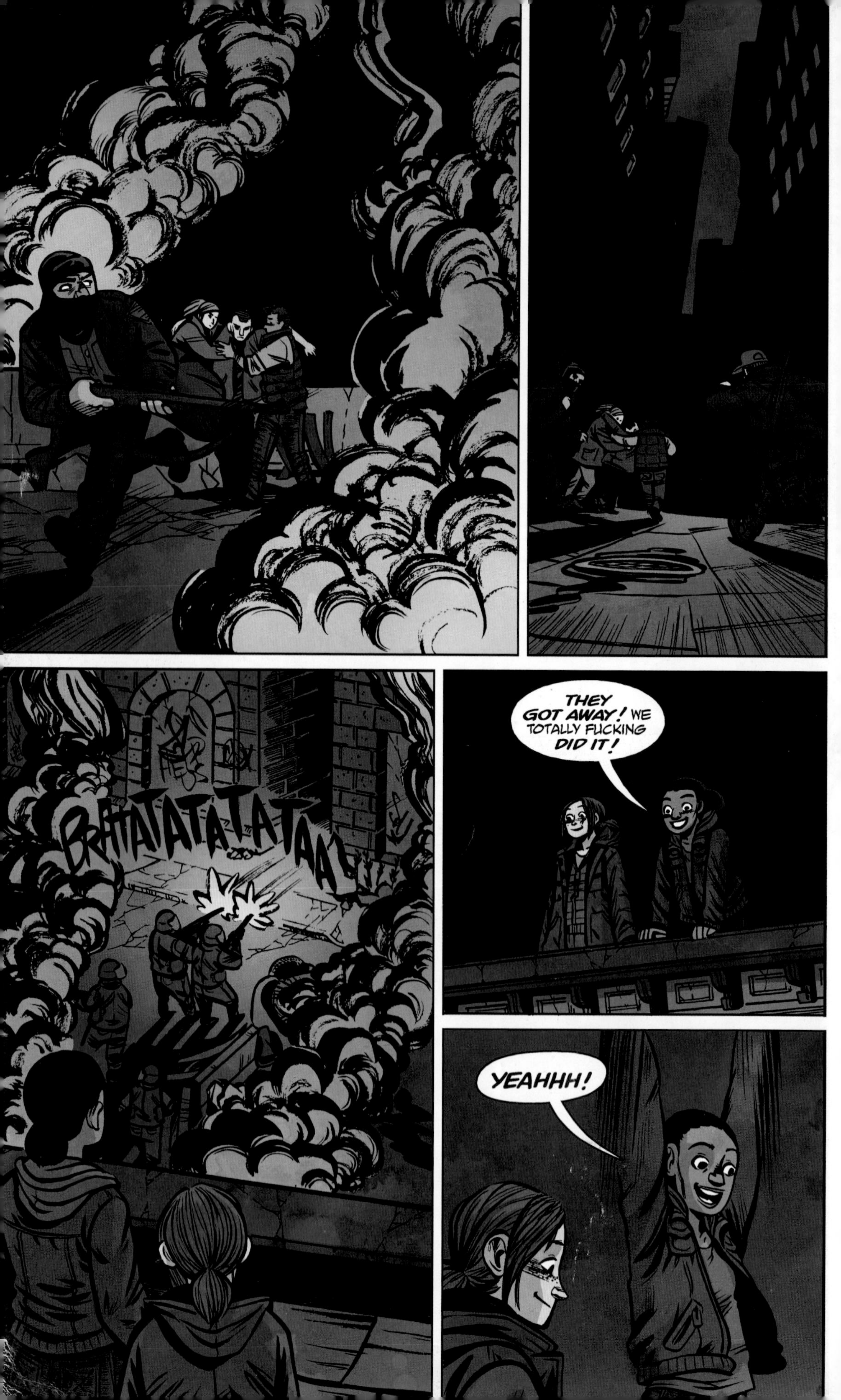
BRATATATATATAA!
THEY GOT AWAY! WE TOTALLY FUCKING DID IT!
YEAHHH!

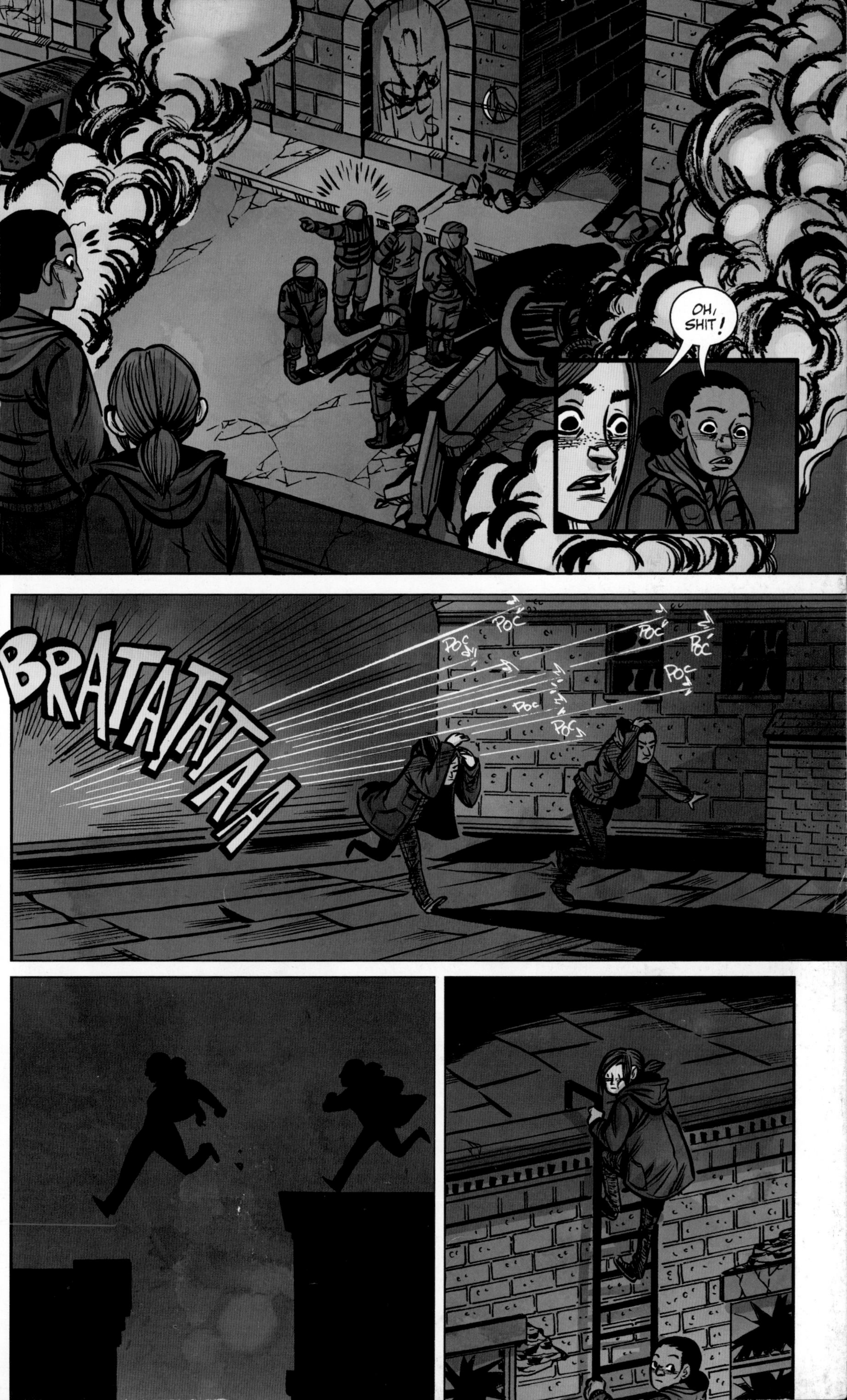
OH, SHIT!
BRATATATAA
POC
POC
POC
POC
POC
POC
POC

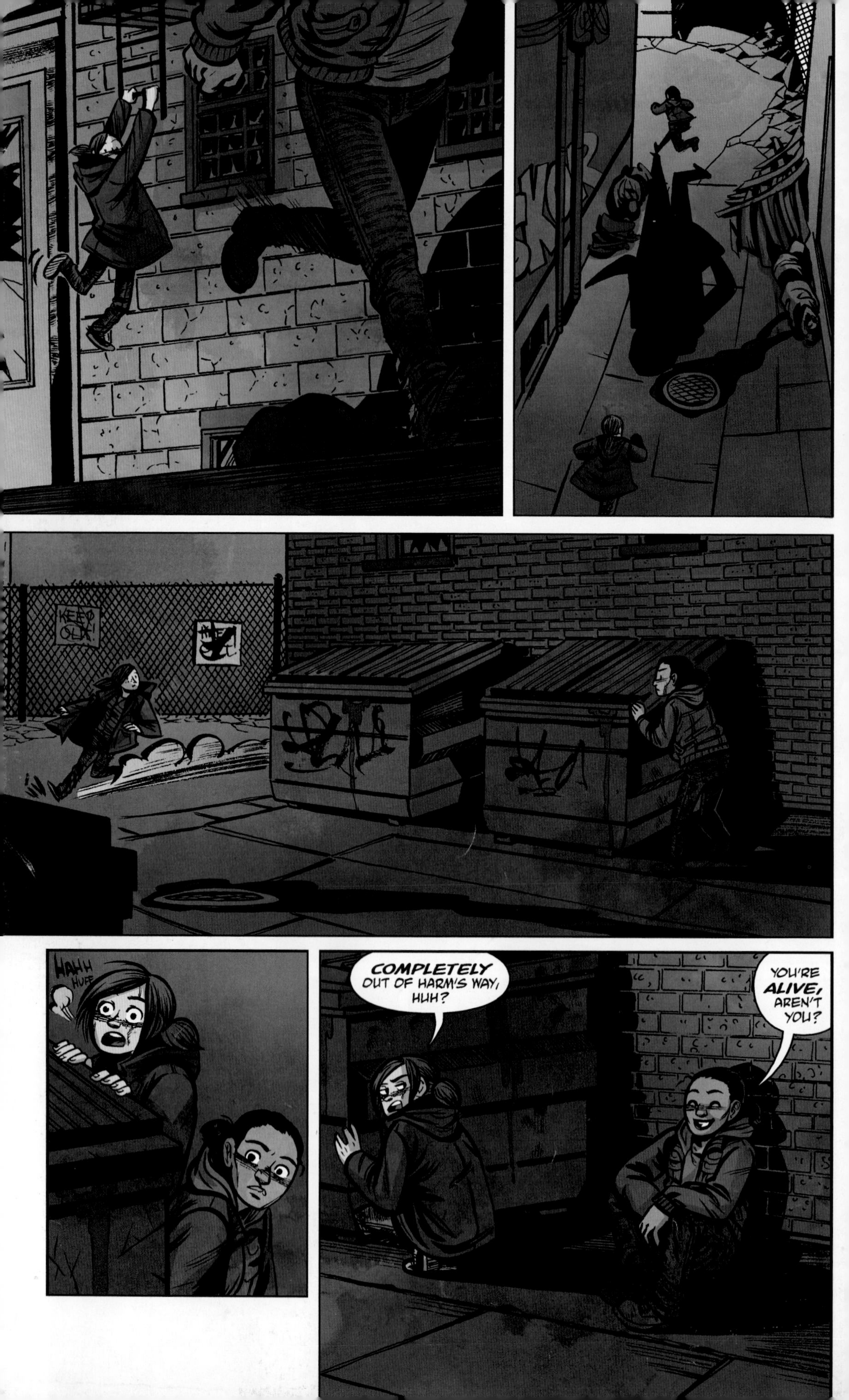
HAHH
HUFF
COMPLETELY OUT OF HARM'S WAY, HUH?
YOU'RE ALIVE, AREN'T YOU?

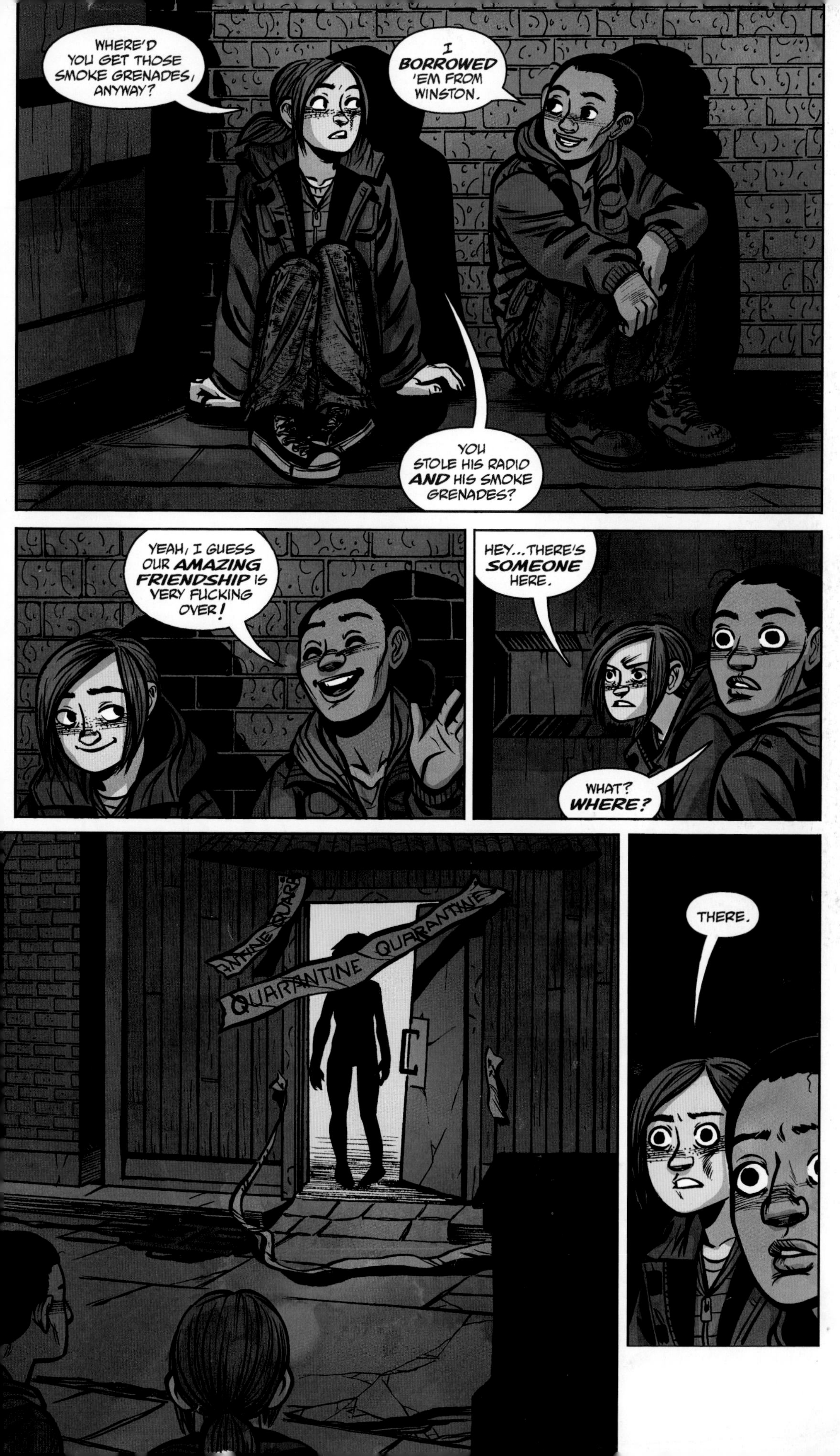
WHERE'D YOU GET THOSE SMOKE GRENADES, ANYWAY?
I BORROWED 'EM FROM WINSTON.
YOU STOLE HIS RADIO AND HIS SMOKE GRENADES?
YEAH, I GUESS OUR AMAZING FRIENDSHIP IS VERY FUCKING OVER!
HEY...THERE'S SOMEONE HERE.
WHAT? WHERE?
QUARANTINE
QUARANTINE
THERE.

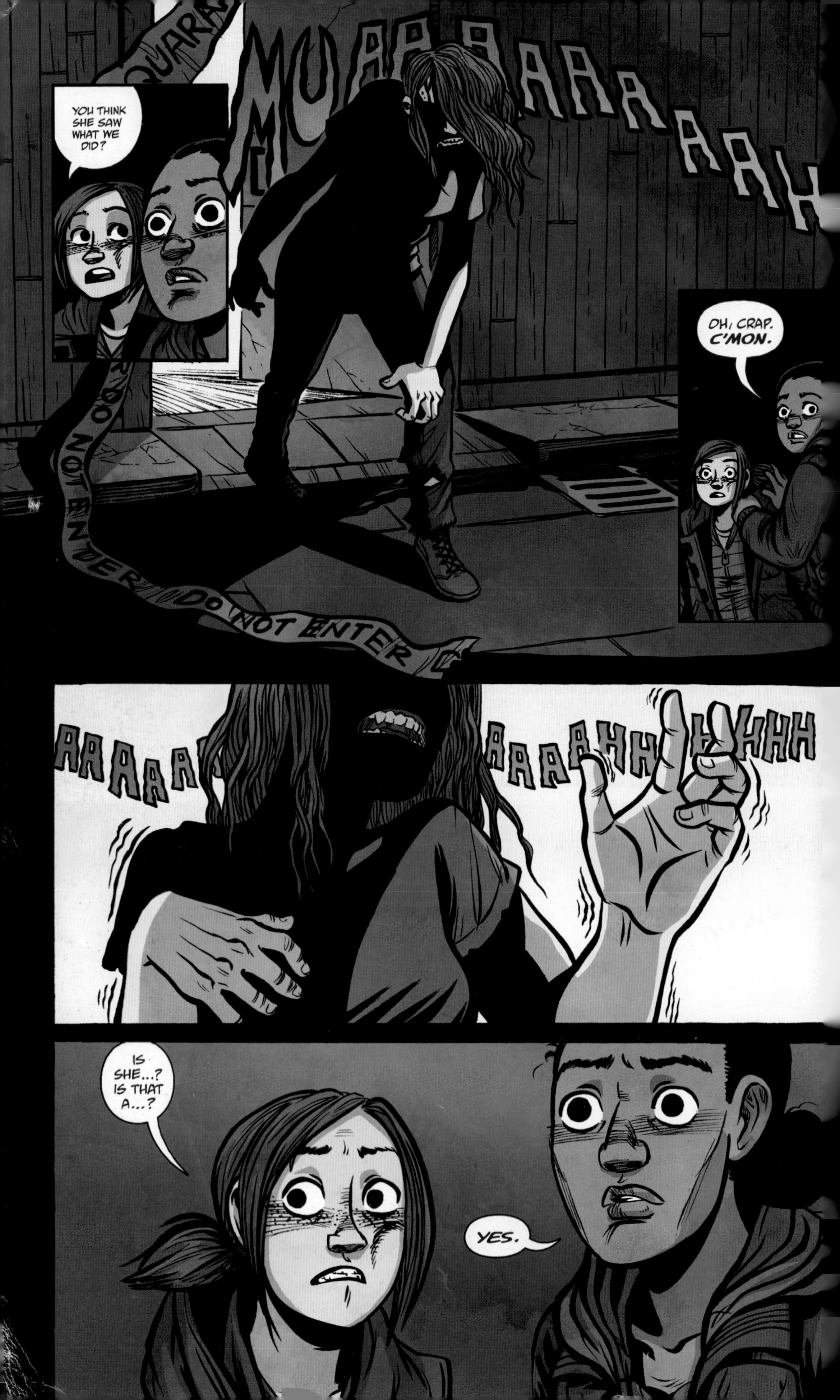
QUARA
MUAAAAAAAAAAAAH
YOU THINK SHE SAW WHAT WE DID?
DO NOT ENTER
DO NOT ENTER
OH, CRAP. C'MON.
AAAAAAAAAAAAHHHHHH
IS SHE...? IS THAT A...?
YES.

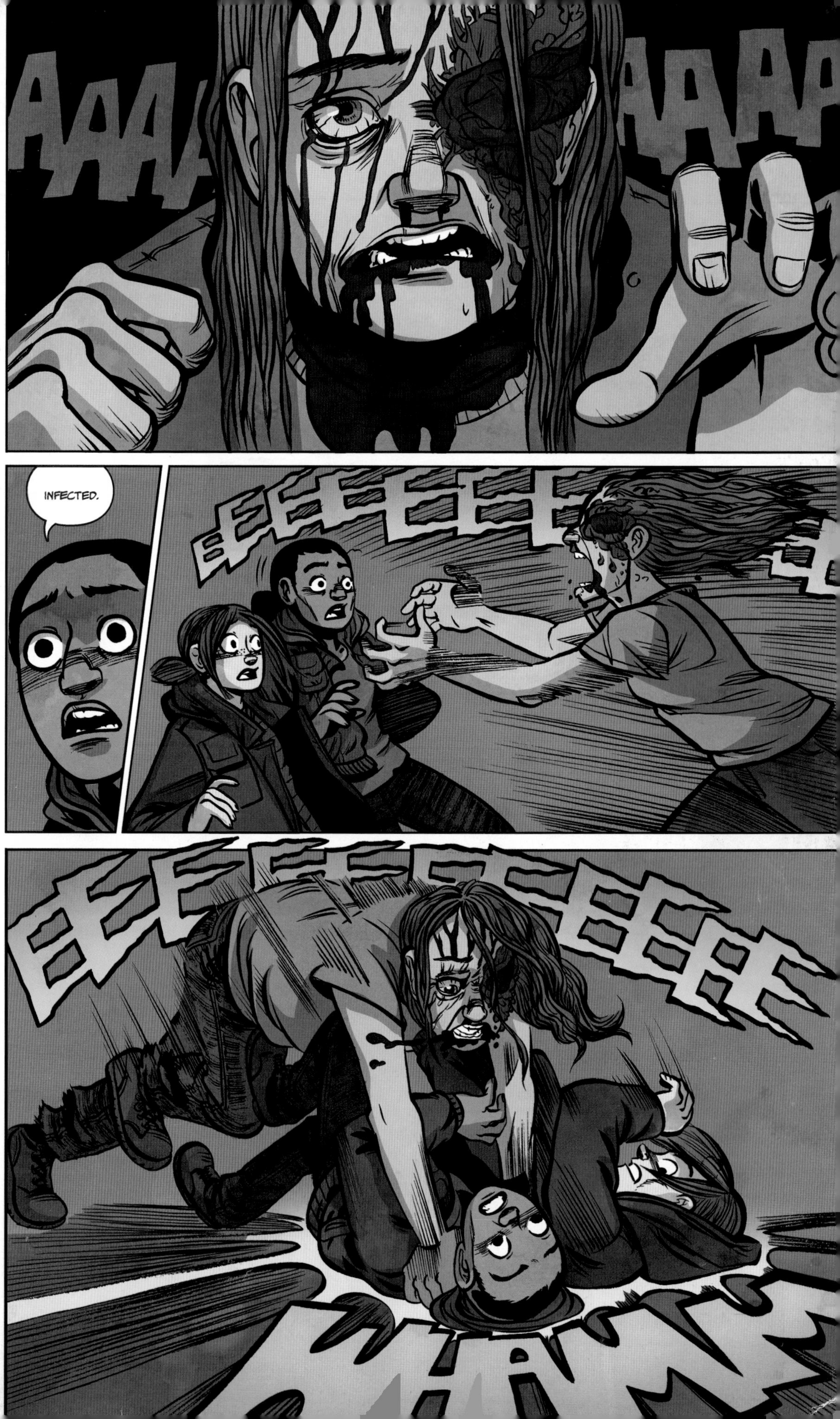
AAAAAAAA
INFECTED.
EEEEEEEE
EEEEEEEEEE
WHAM

SCREEEAM

KLAK
KLAK

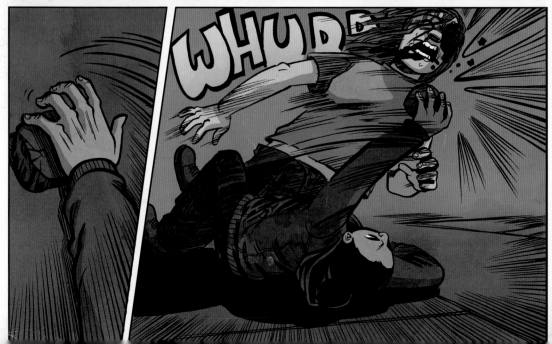

WHUD

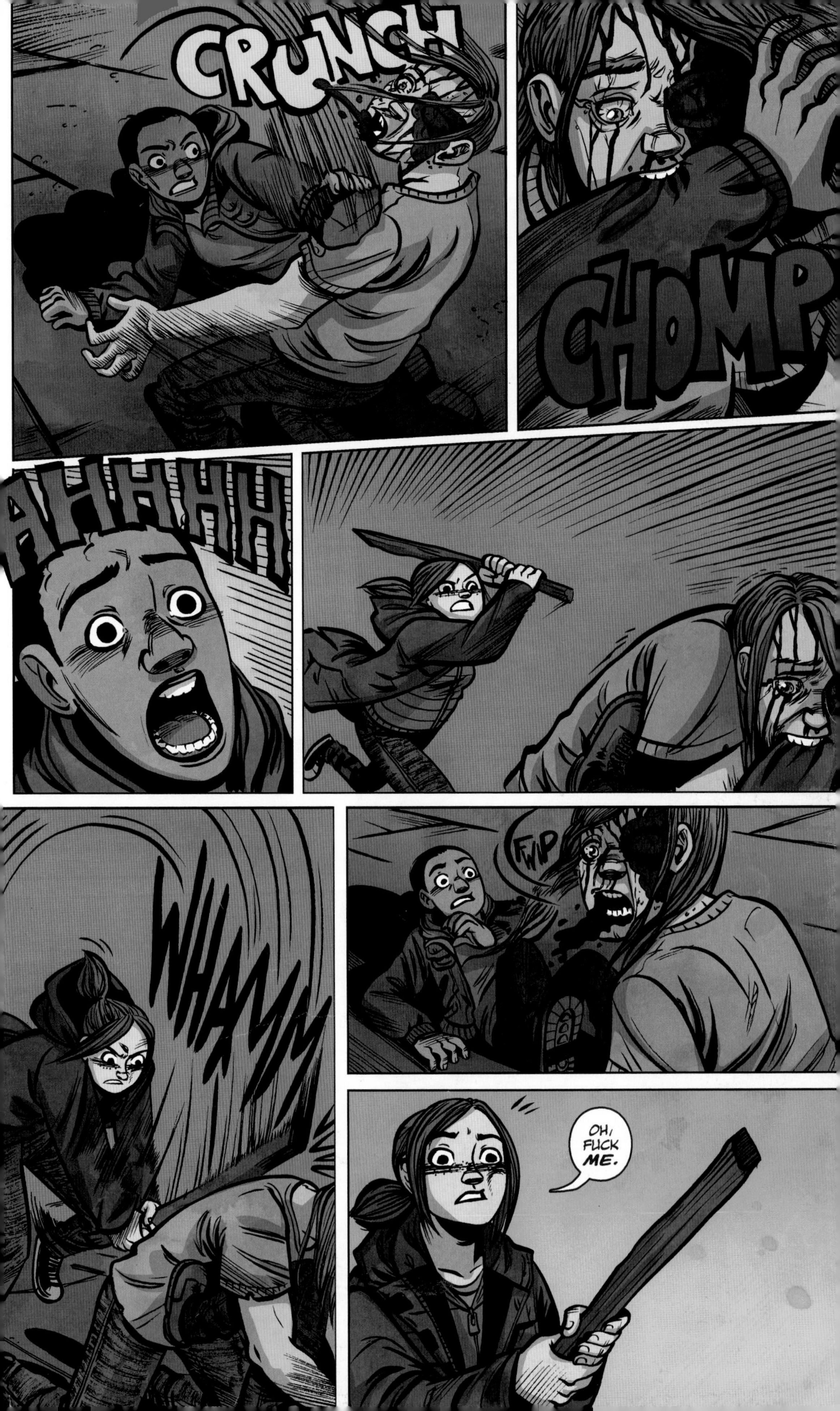

CRUNCH
CHOMP
AHHHHH
WHAMM
FWIP
OH, FUCK ME.

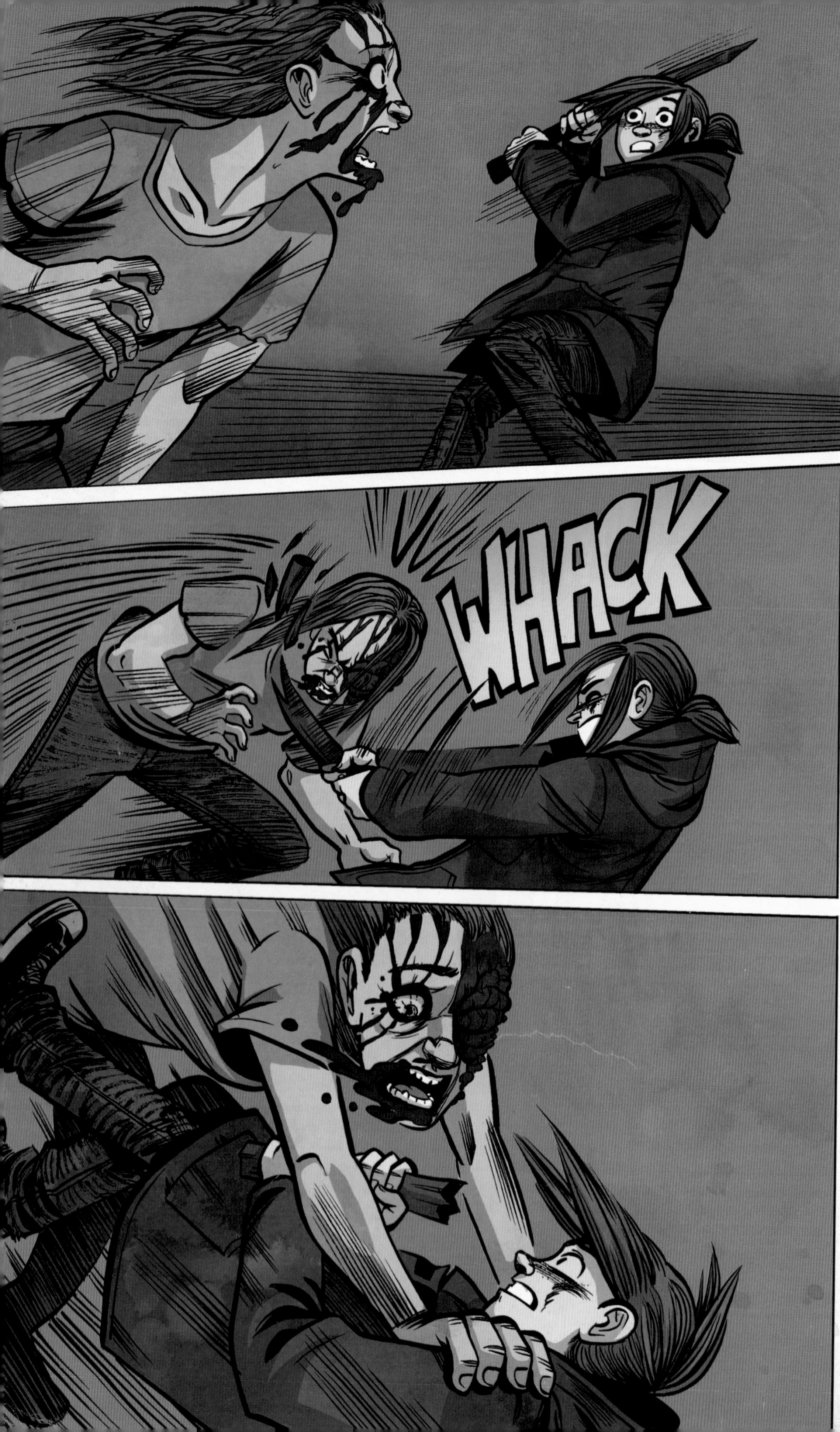
WHACK

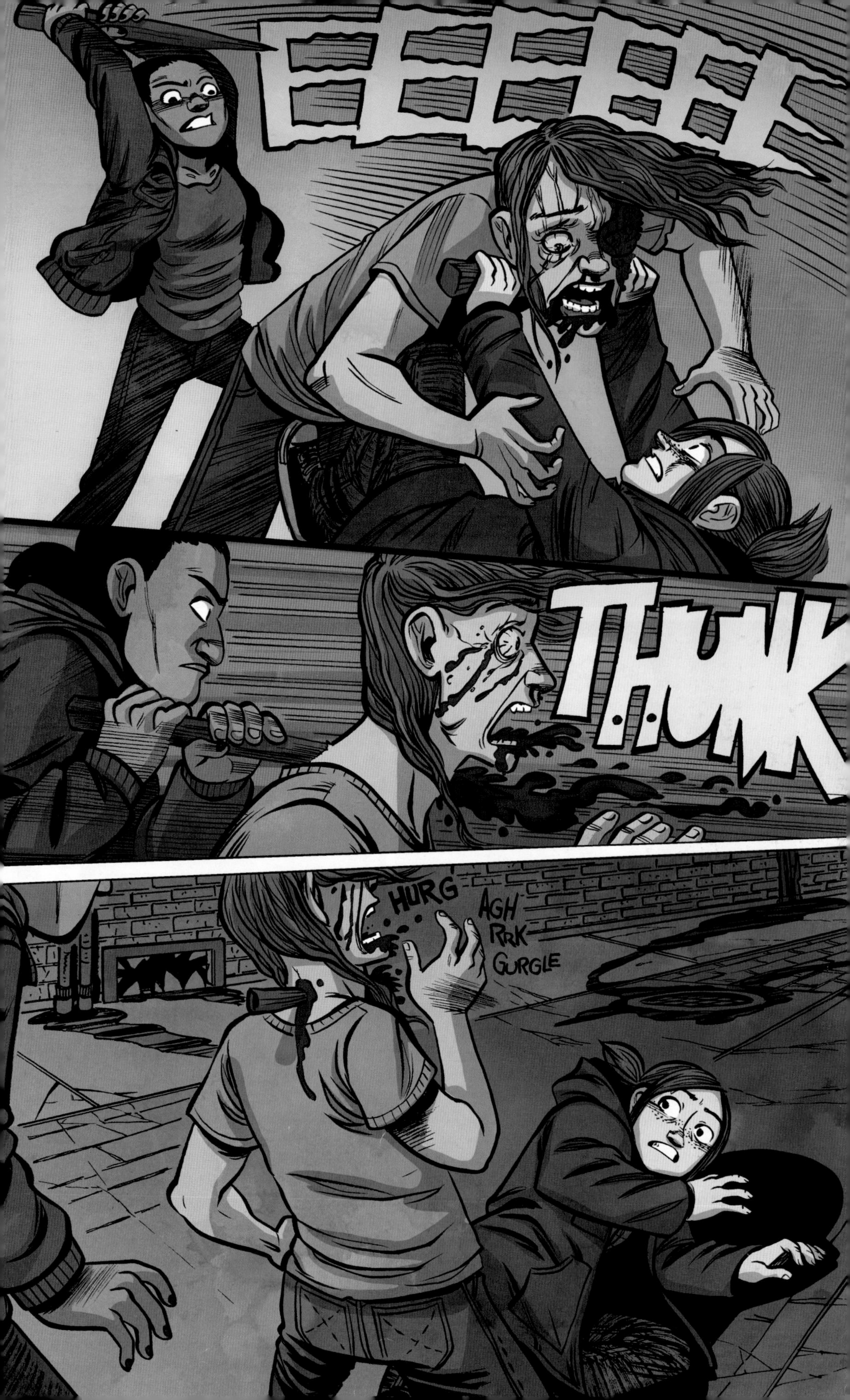
EEEEEK
THUNK
HURG
AGH
RRK
GURGLE

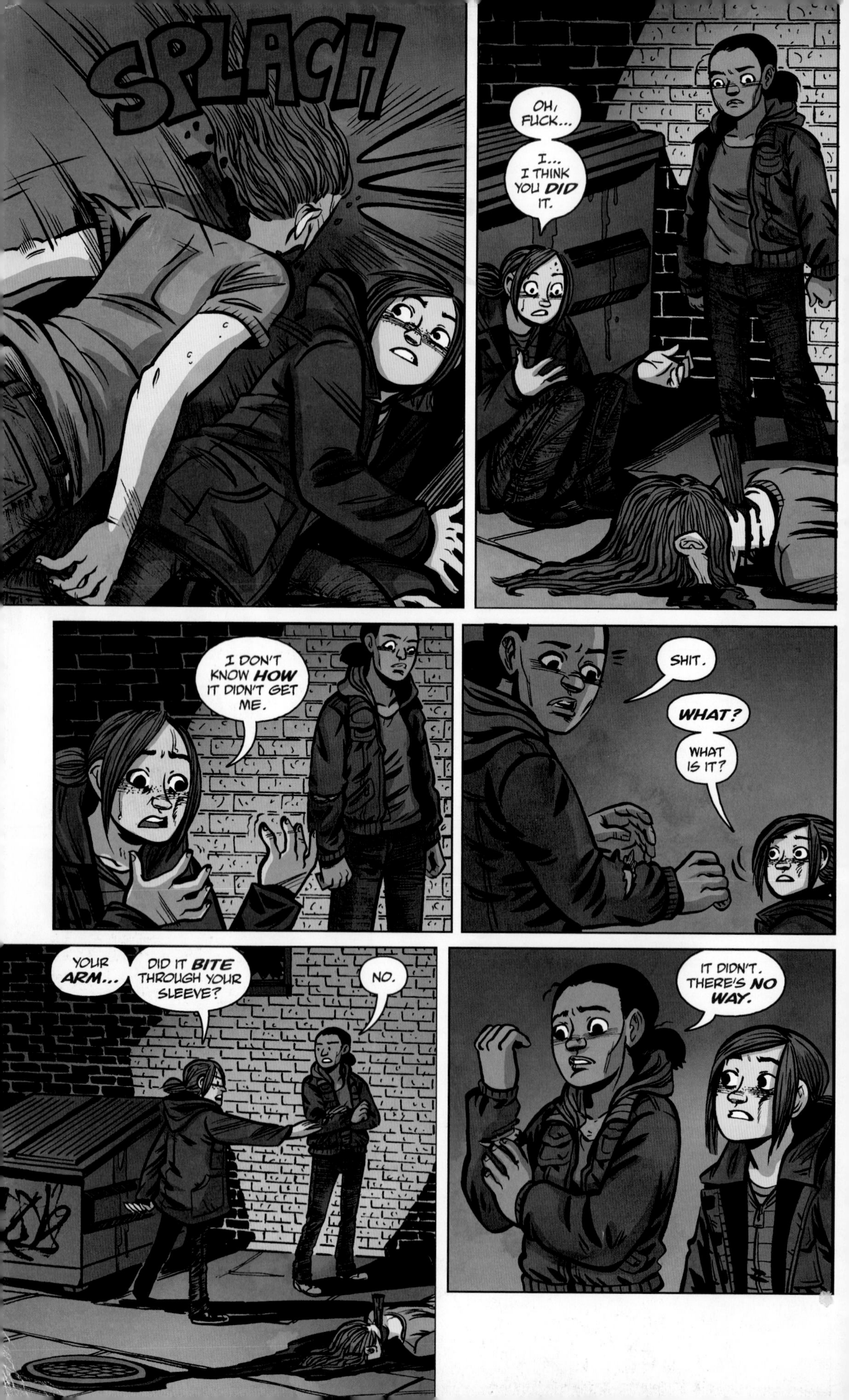
SPLACH
OH, FUCK...
I... I THINK YOU DID IT.
I DON'T KNOW HOW IT DIDN'T GET ME.
SHIT.
WHAT?
WHAT IS IT?
YOUR ARM...
DID IT BITE THROUGH YOUR SLEEVE?
NO.
IT DIDN'T. THERE'S NO WAY.

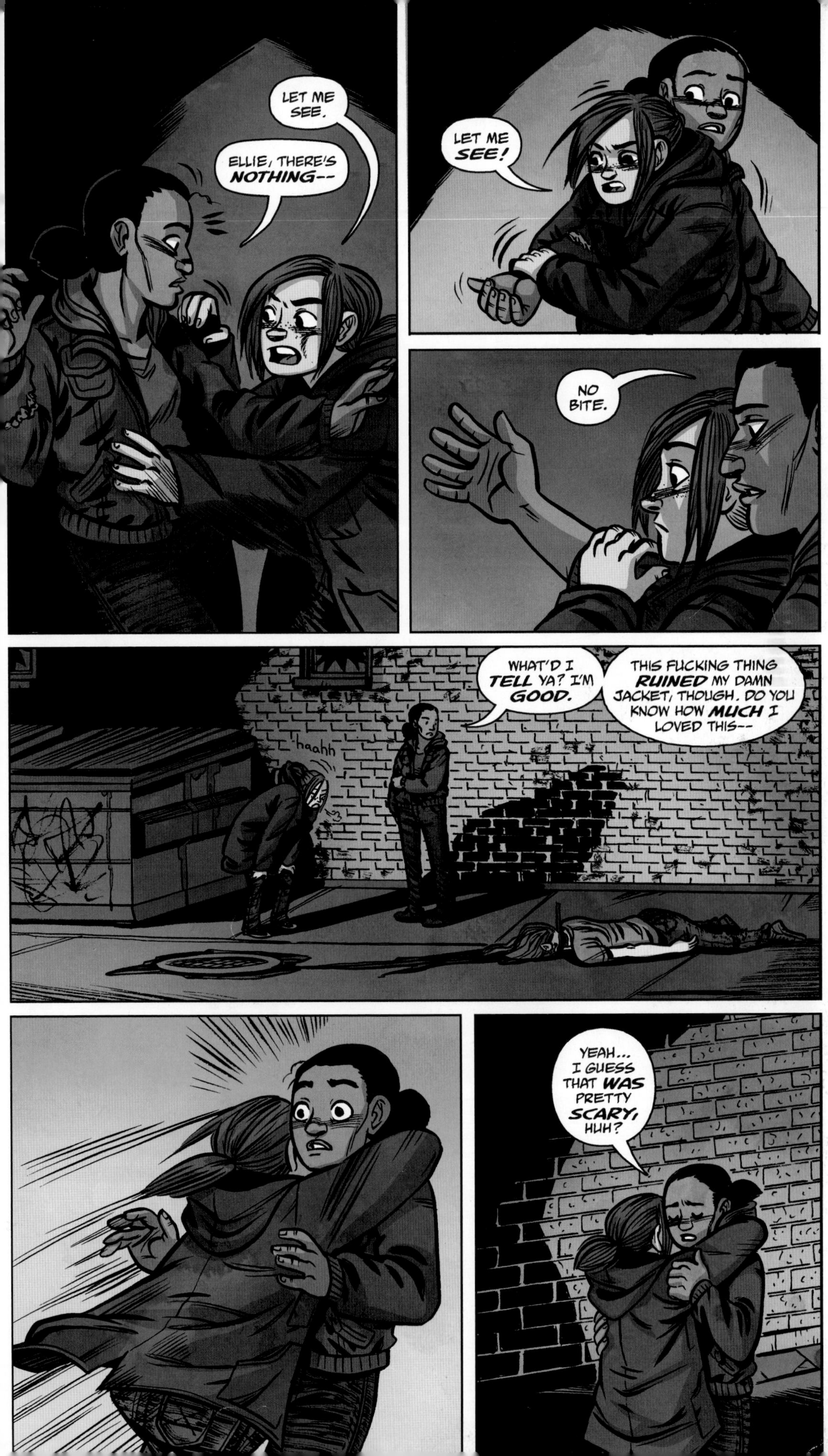

LET ME SEE.
ELLIE, THERE'S NOTHING--
LET ME SEE!
NO BITE.
WHAT'D I TELL YA? I'M GOOD.
THIS FUCKING THING RUINED MY DAMN JACKET, THOUGH. DO YOU KNOW HOW MUCH I LOVED THIS--
haahh
YEAH... I GUESS THAT WAS PRETTY SCARY, HUH?

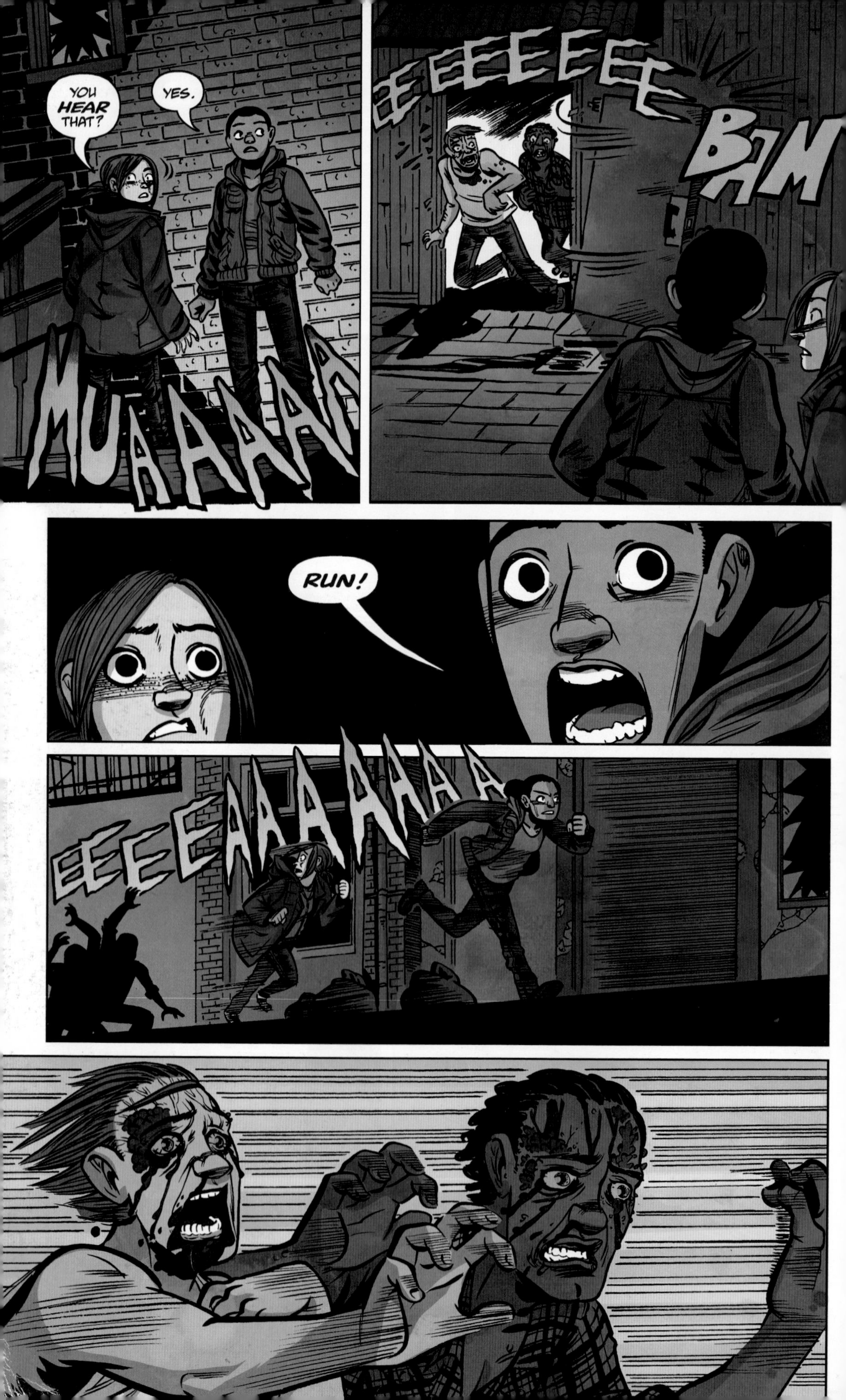
YOU HEAR THAT?
YES.
MUAAAAA
EEEEEEEE
BAM
RUN!
EEEEAAAAAAAA

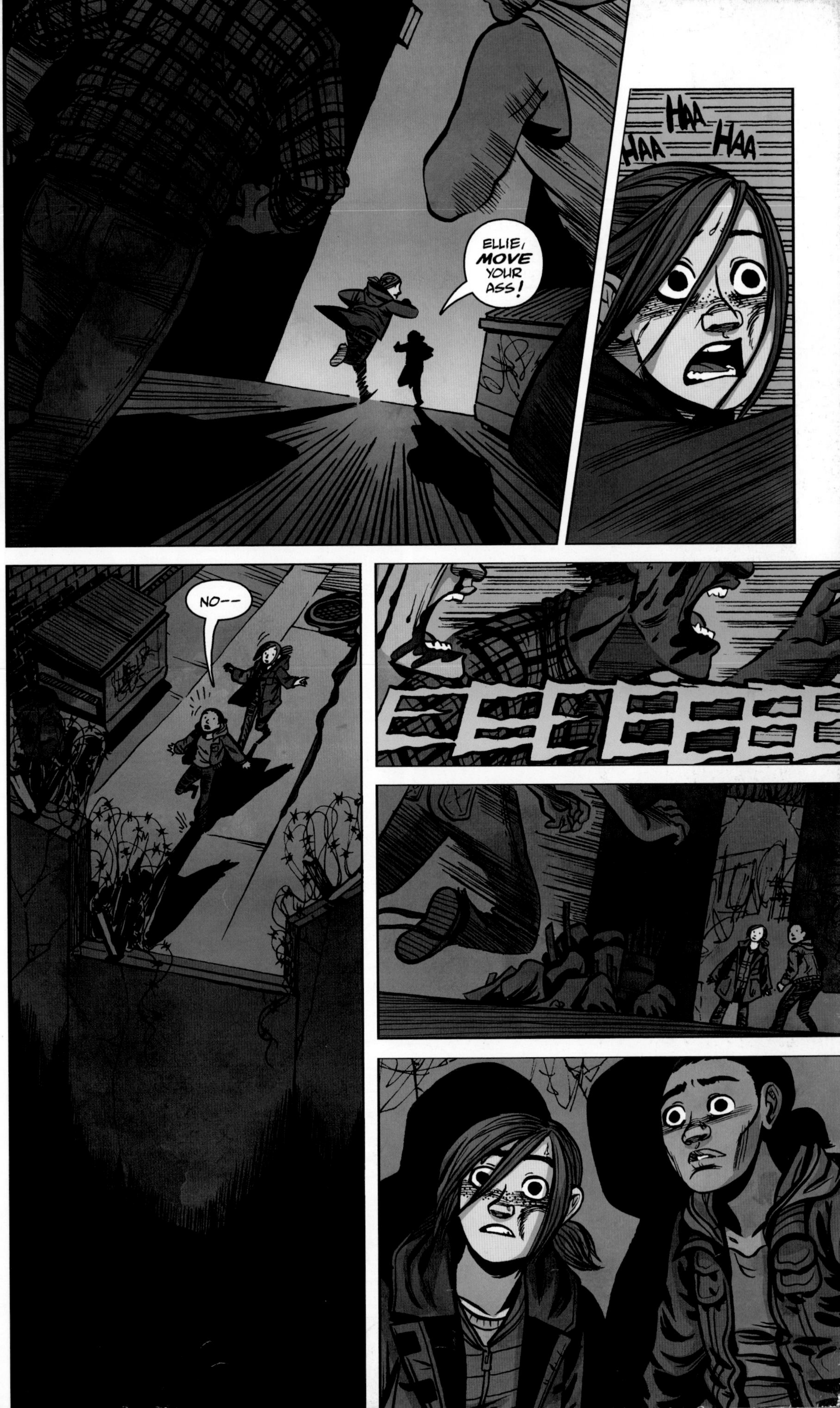
ELLIE, MOVE YOUR ASS!
HAA HAA HAA
NO--
EEEEEEEE

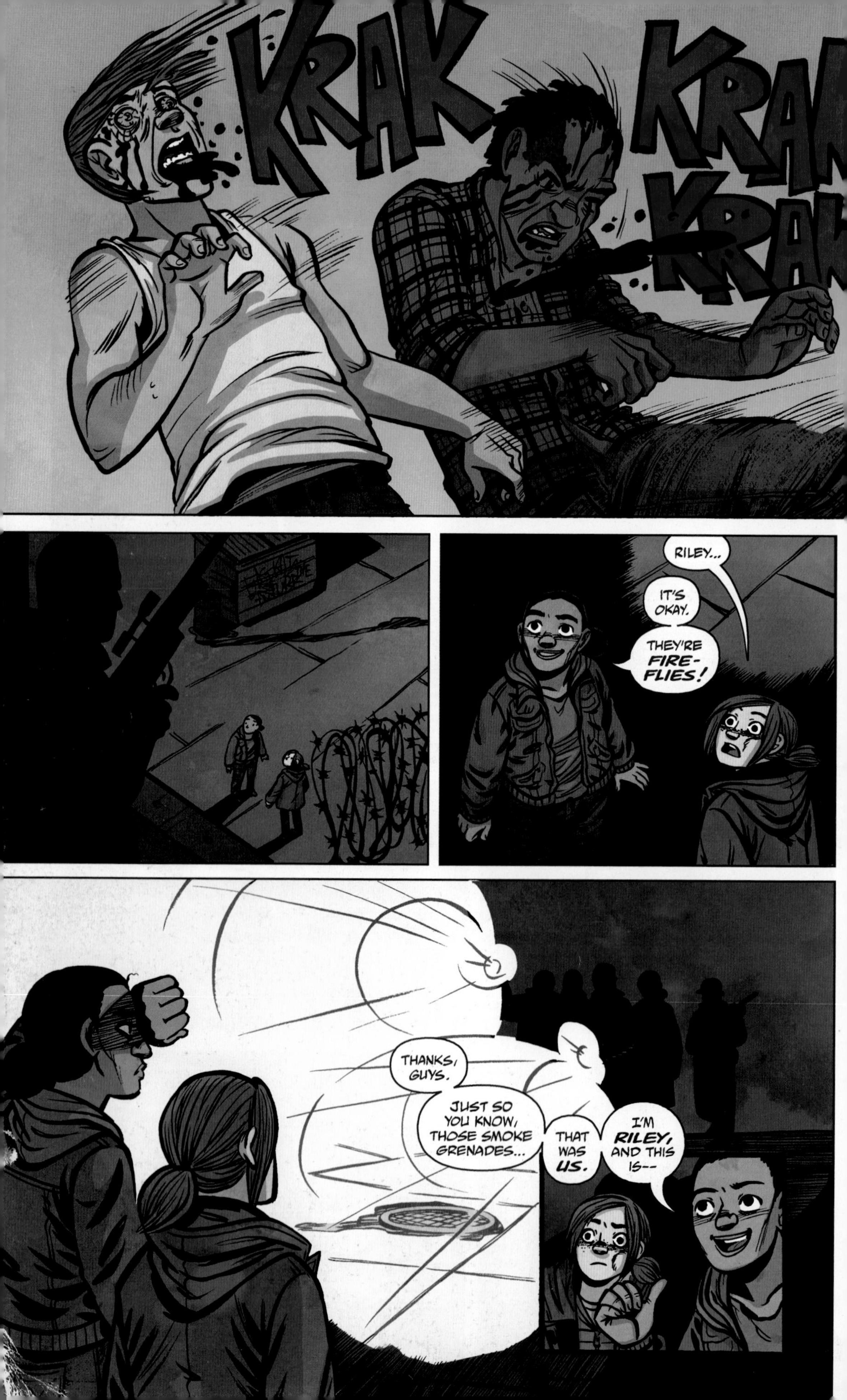
KRAK
KRAK
KRAK
RILEY...
IT'S OKAY.
THEY'RE FIRE-FLIES!
THANKS, GUYS.
JUST SO YOU KNOW, THOSE SMOKE GRENADES...
THAT WAS US.
I'M RILEY, AND THIS IS--

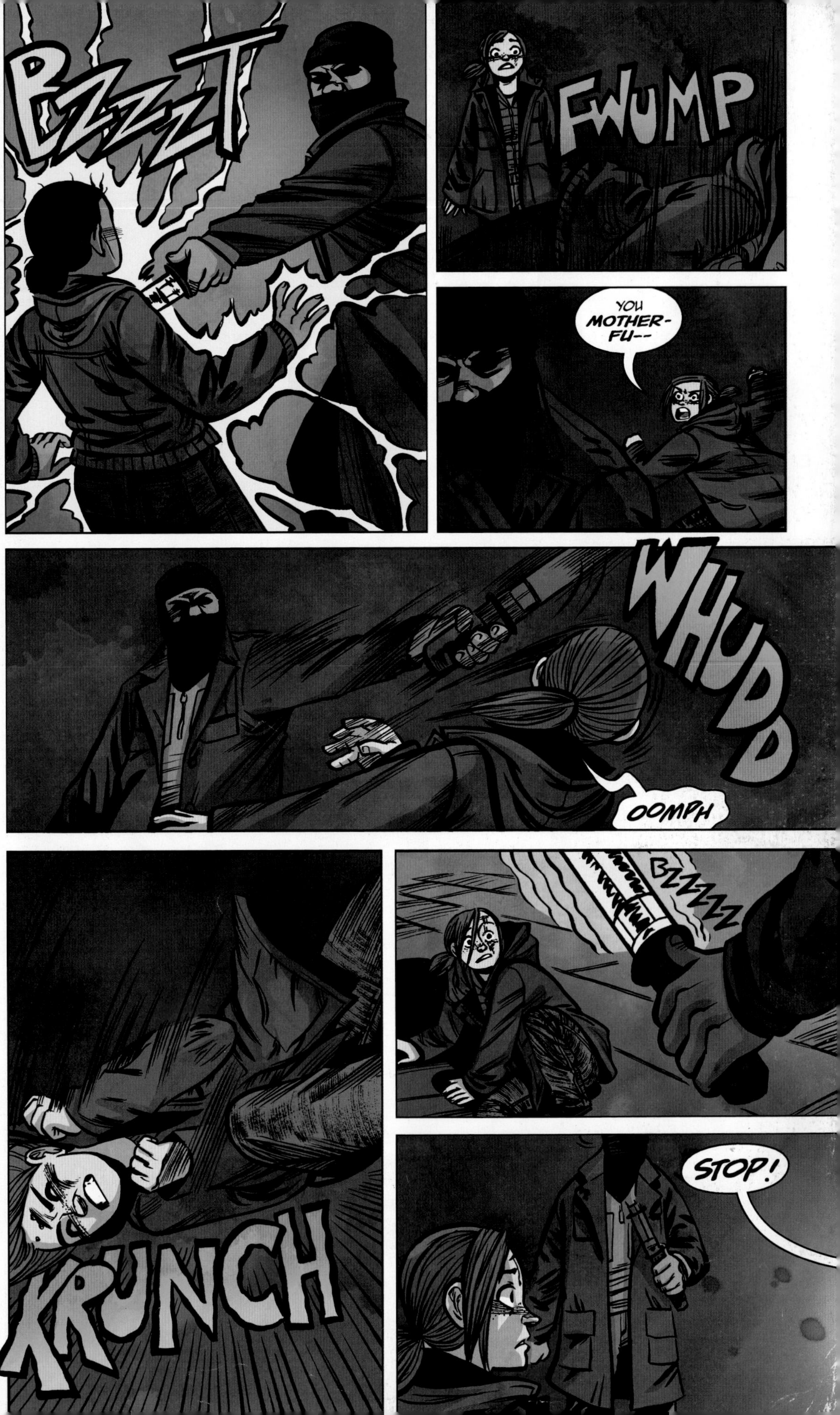
BZZZZT
FWUMP
YOU MOTHER-FU--
WHUDD
OOMPH
KRUNCH
BZZZZZ
STOP!

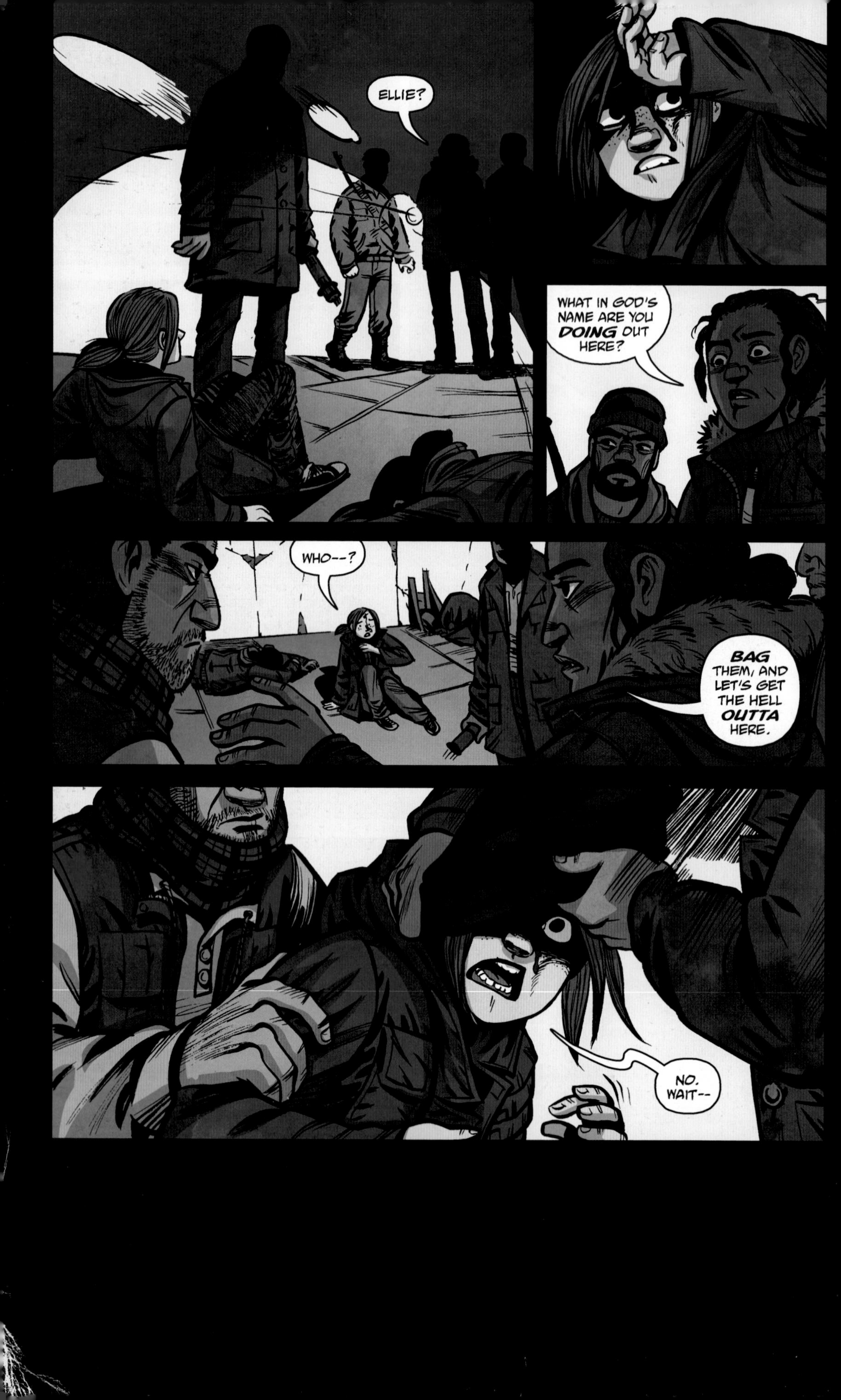
ELLIE?
WHAT IN GOD'S NAME ARE YOU DOING OUT HERE?
WHO--?
BAG THEM, AND LET'S GET THE HELL OUTTA HERE.
NO. WAIT--

CHAPTER FOUR

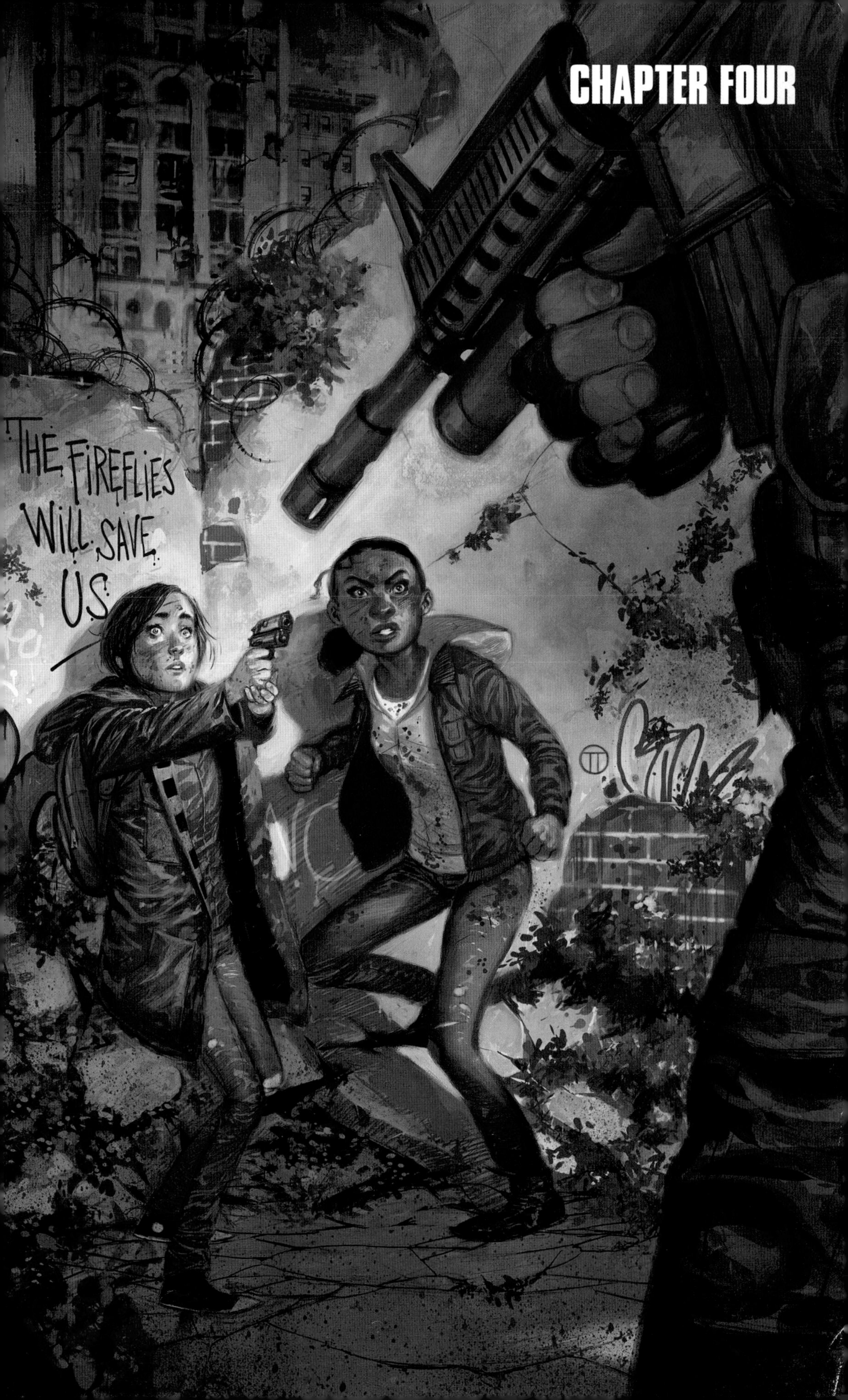

THE FIREFLIES WILL SAVE US

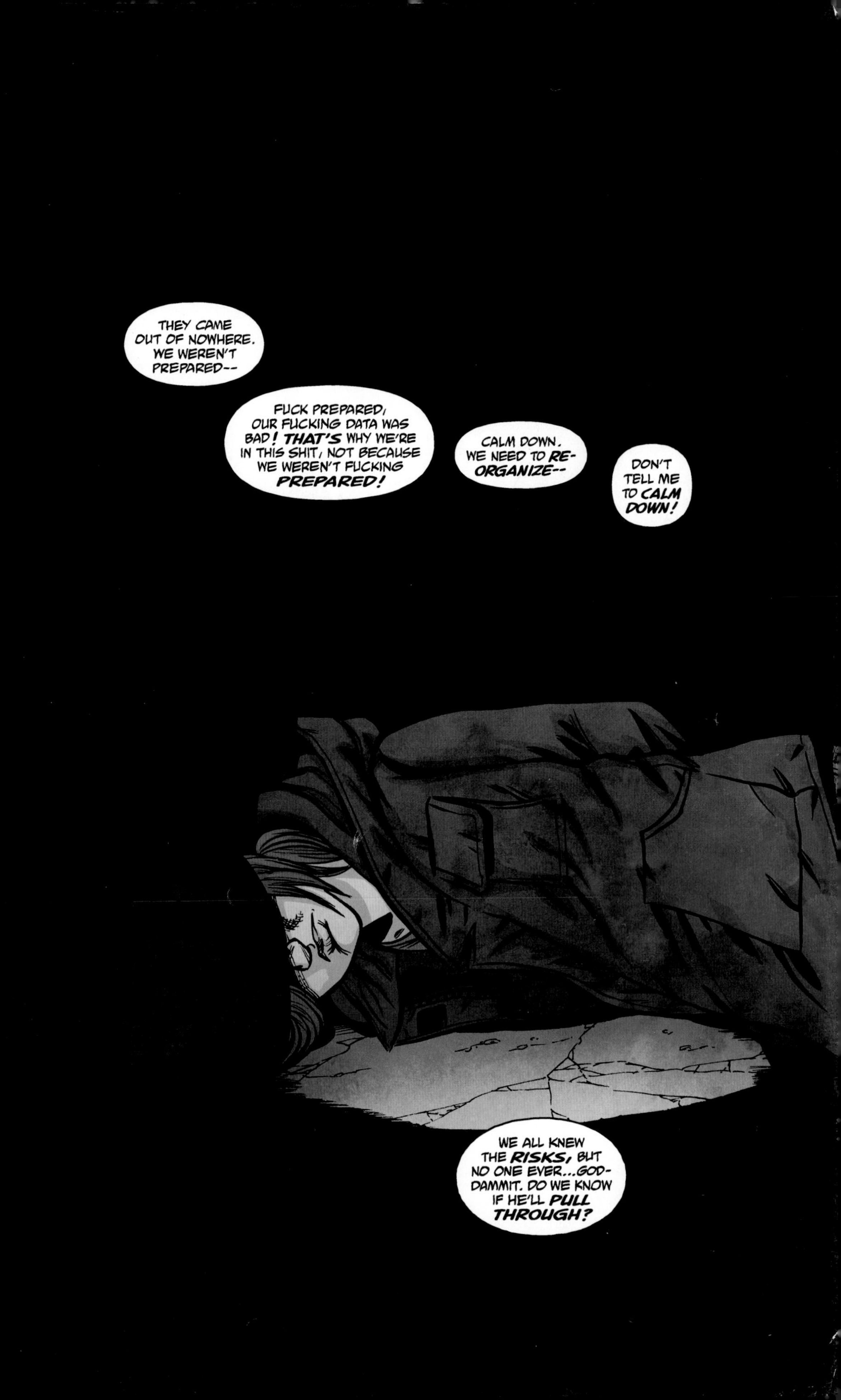
THEY CAME OUT OF NOWHERE. WE WEREN'T PREPARED--
FUCK PREPARED, OUR FUCKING DATA WAS BAD! THAT'S WHY WE'RE IN THIS SHIT, NOT BECAUSE WE WEREN'T FUCKING PREPARED!
CALM DOWN. WE NEED TO RE-ORGANIZE--
DON'T TELL ME TO CALM DOWN!
WE ALL KNEW THE RISKS, BUT NO ONE EVER...GOD-DAMMIT. DO WE KNOW IF HE'LL PULL THROUGH?

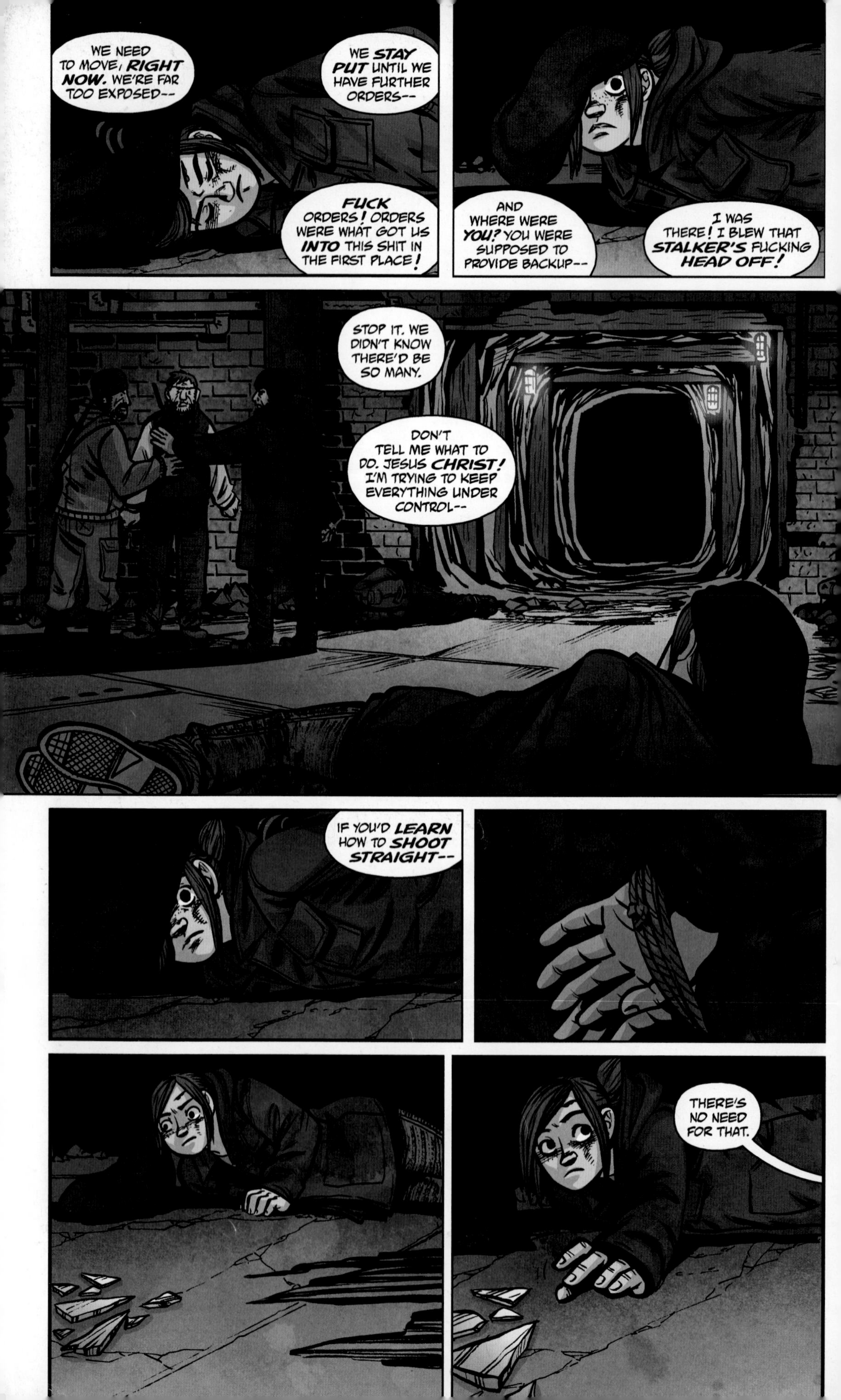

WE NEED TO MOVE, RIGHT NOW. WE'RE FAR TOO EXPOSED--
WE STAY PUT UNTIL WE HAVE FURTHER ORDERS--
FUCK ORDERS! ORDERS WERE WHAT GOT US INTO THIS SHIT IN THE FIRST PLACE!
AND WHERE WERE YOU? YOU WERE SUPPOSED TO PROVIDE BACKUP--
I WAS THERE! I BLEW THAT STALKER'S FUCKING HEAD OFF!
STOP IT. WE DIDN'T KNOW THERE'D BE SO MANY.
DON'T TELL ME WHAT TO DO. JESUS CHRIST! I'M TRYING TO KEEP EVERYTHING UNDER CONTROL--
IF YOU'D LEARN HOW TO SHOOT STRAIGHT--
THERE'S NO NEED FOR THAT.

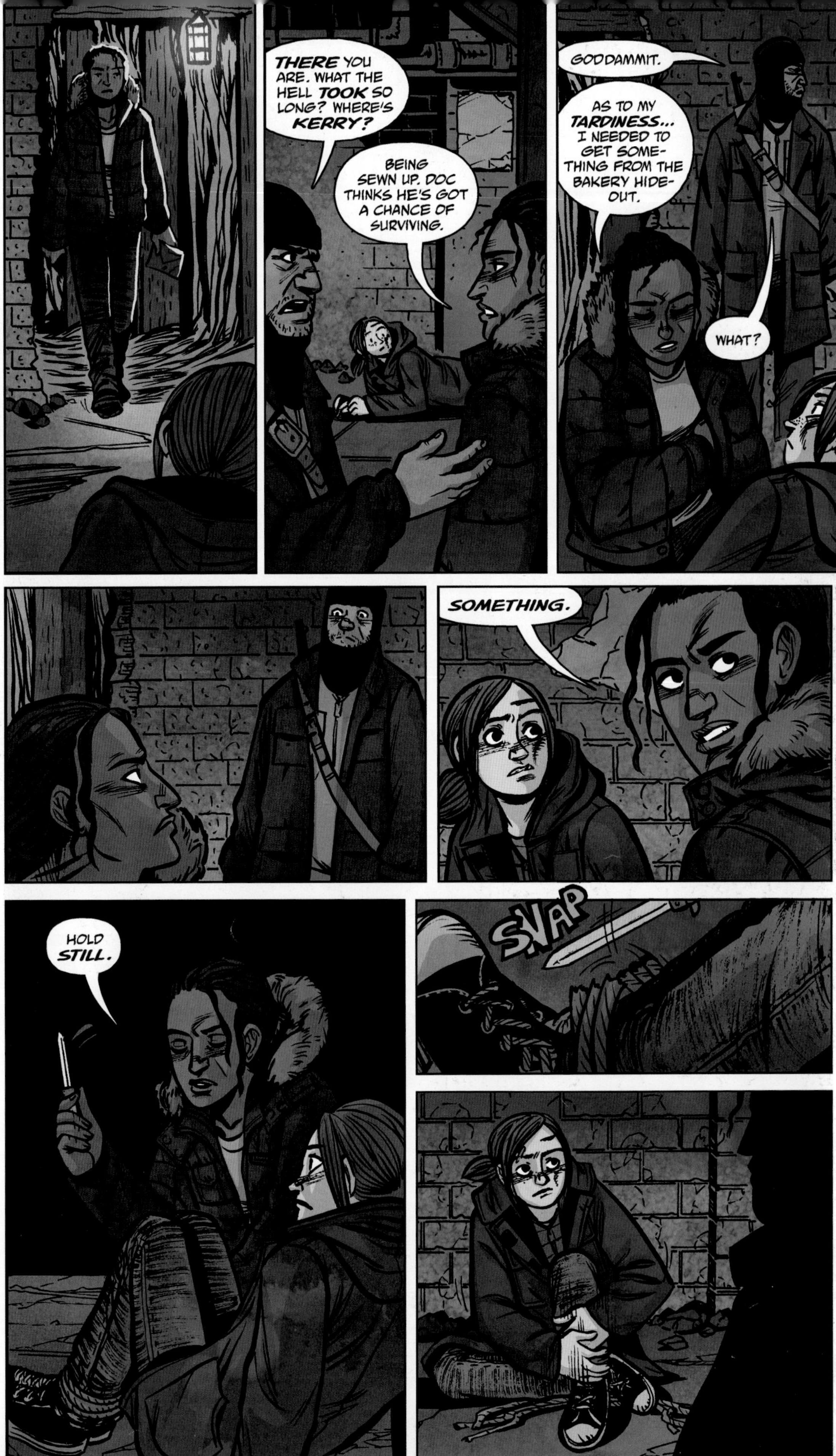
THERE YOU ARE. WHAT THE HELL TOOK SO LONG? WHERE'S KERRY?
BEING SEWN UP. DOC THINKS HE'S GOT A CHANCE OF SURVIVING.
GODDAMMIT.
AS TO MY TARDINESS... I NEEDED TO GET SOMETHING FROM THE BAKERY HIDE-OUT.
WHAT?
SOMETHING.
HOLD STILL.
SNAP

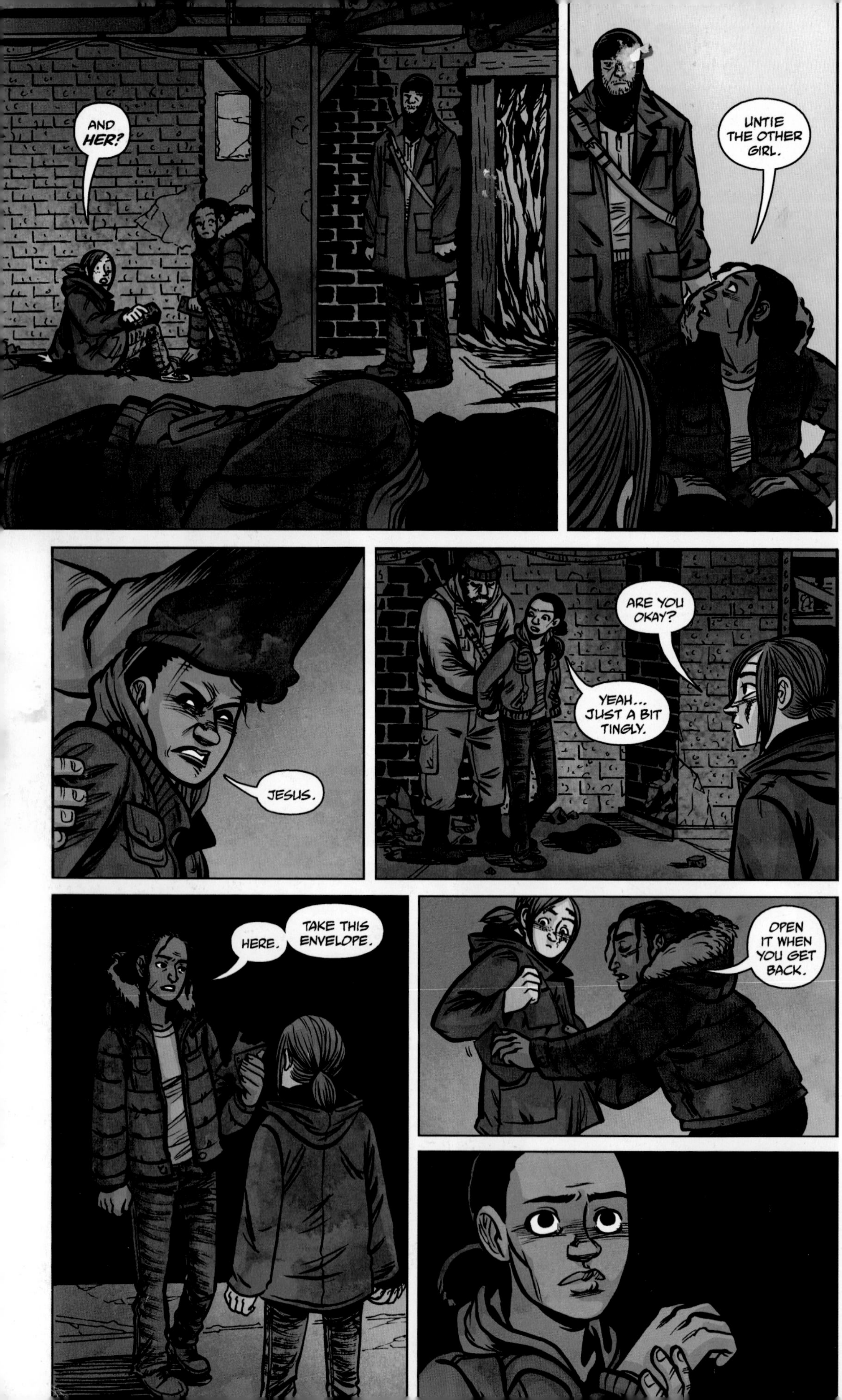
AND HER?
UNTIE THE OTHER GIRL.
JESUS.
ARE YOU OKAY?
YEAH... JUST A BIT TINGLY.
HERE.
TAKE THIS ENVELOPE.
OPEN IT WHEN YOU GET BACK.

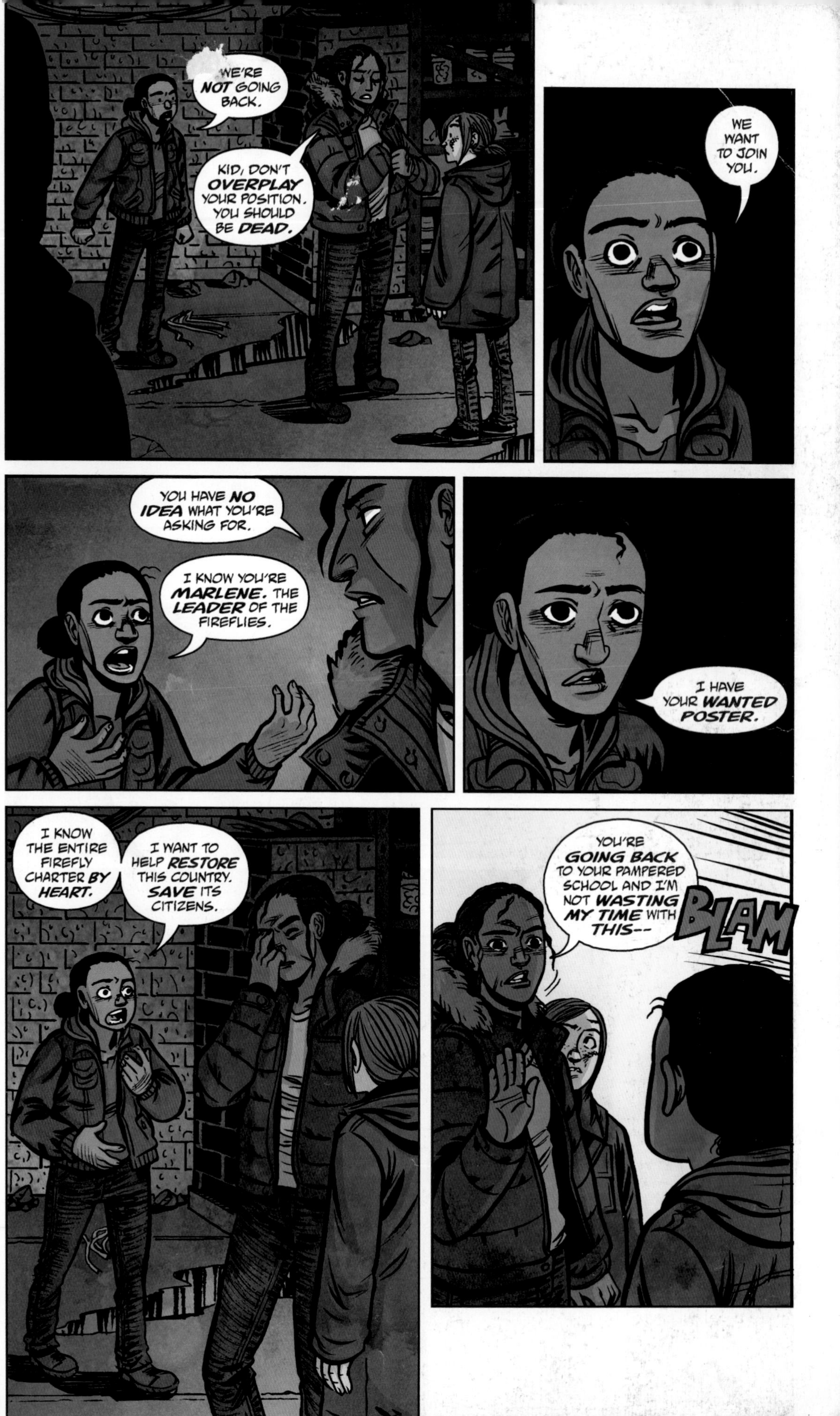
WE'RE NOT GOING BACK.
KID, DON'T OVERPLAY YOUR POSITION. YOU SHOULD BE DEAD.
WE WANT TO JOIN YOU.
YOU HAVE NO IDEA WHAT YOU'RE ASKING FOR.
I KNOW YOU'RE MARLENE. THE LEADER OF THE FIREFLIES.
I HAVE YOUR WANTED POSTER.
I KNOW THE ENTIRE FIREFLY CHARTER BY HEART.
I WANT TO HELP RESTORE THIS COUNTRY. SAVE ITS CITIZENS.
YOU'RE GOING BACK TO YOUR PAMPERED SCHOOL AND I'M NOT WASTING MY TIME WITH THIS--
BLAM

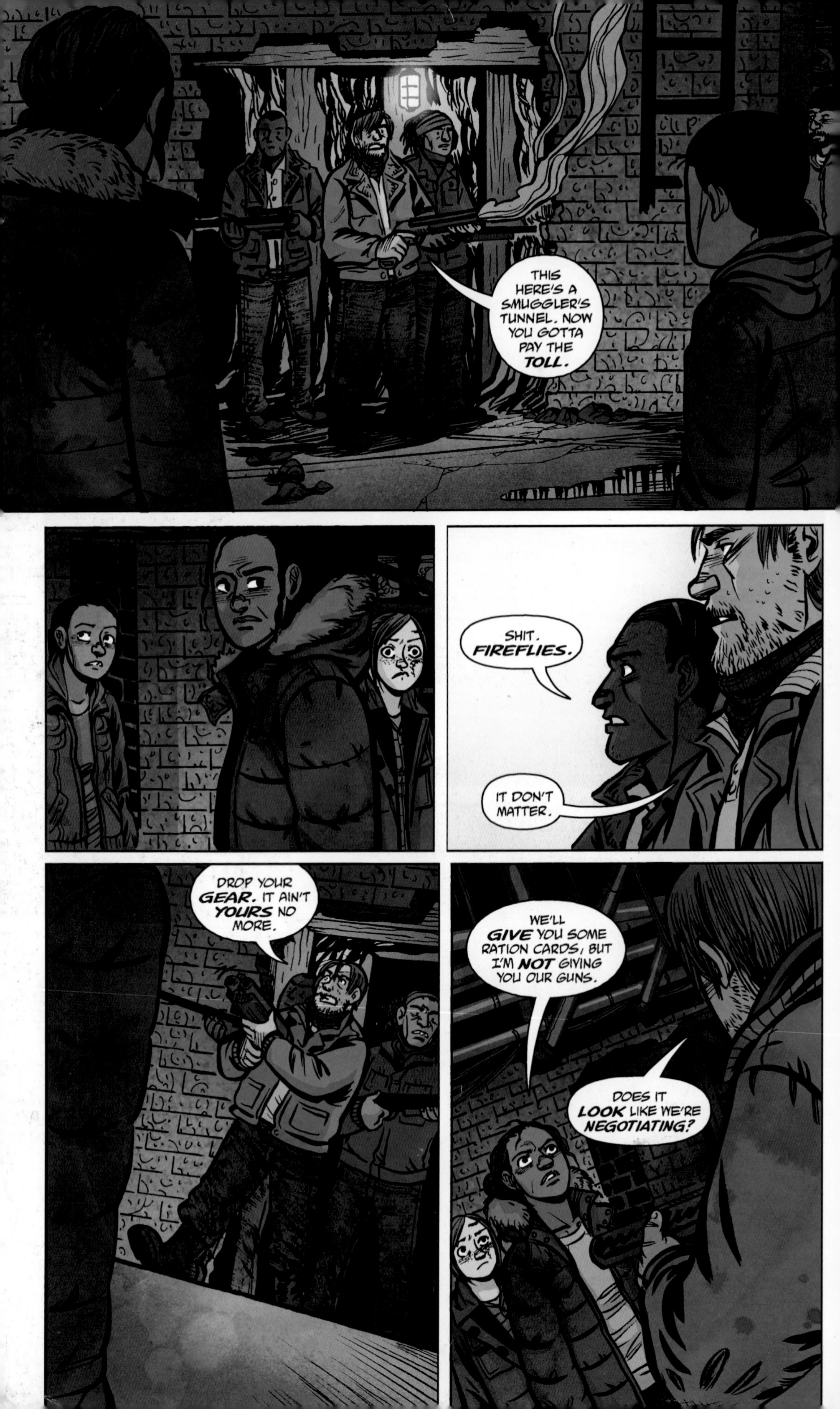
THIS HERE'S A SMUGGLER'S TUNNEL. NOW YOU GOTTA PAY THE TOLL.
SHIT. FIREFLIES.
IT DON'T MATTER.
DROP YOUR GEAR. IT AIN'T YOURS NO MORE.
WE'LL GIVE YOU SOME RATION CARDS, BUT I'M NOT GIVING YOU OUR GUNS.
DOES IT LOOK LIKE WE'RE NEGOTIATING?

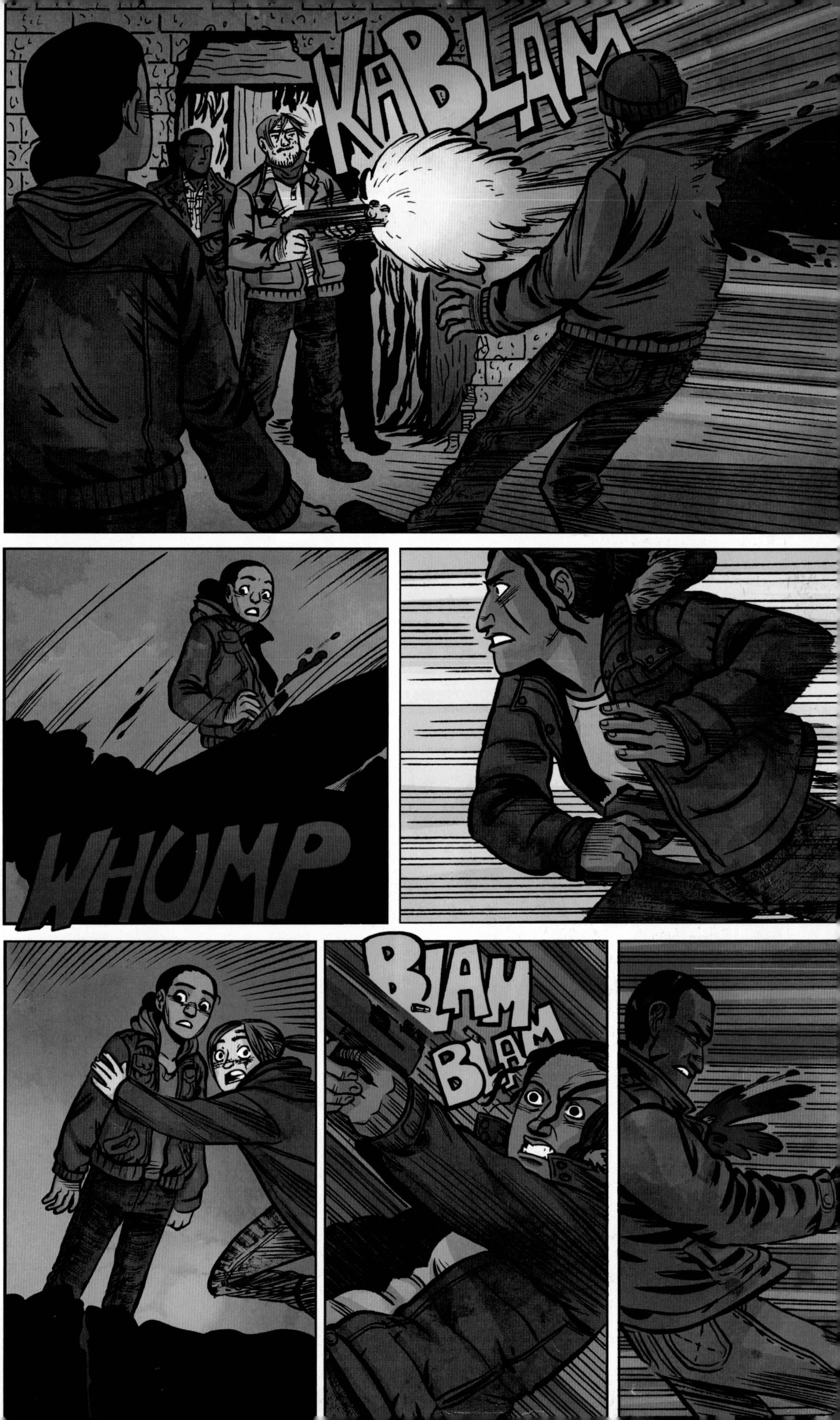
KABLAM
WHUMP
BLAM
BLAM

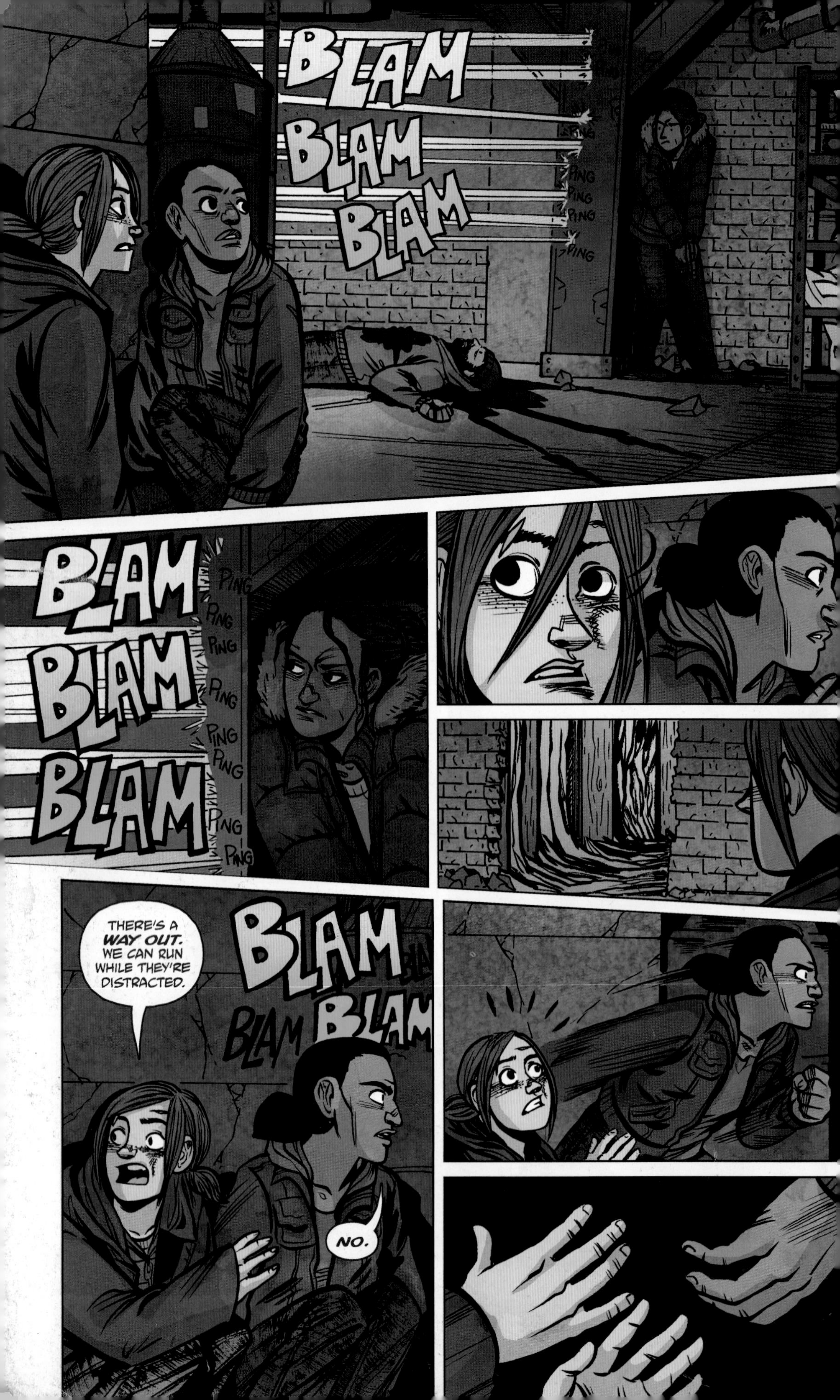
BLAM
BLAM
BLAM
PING
PING
PING
PING
PING
BLAM
BLAM
BLAM
PING
PING
PING
PING
PING
PING
PING
PING
THERE'S A WAY OUT. WE CAN RUN WHILE THEY'RE DISTRACTED.
BLAM
BLAM BLAM
NO.

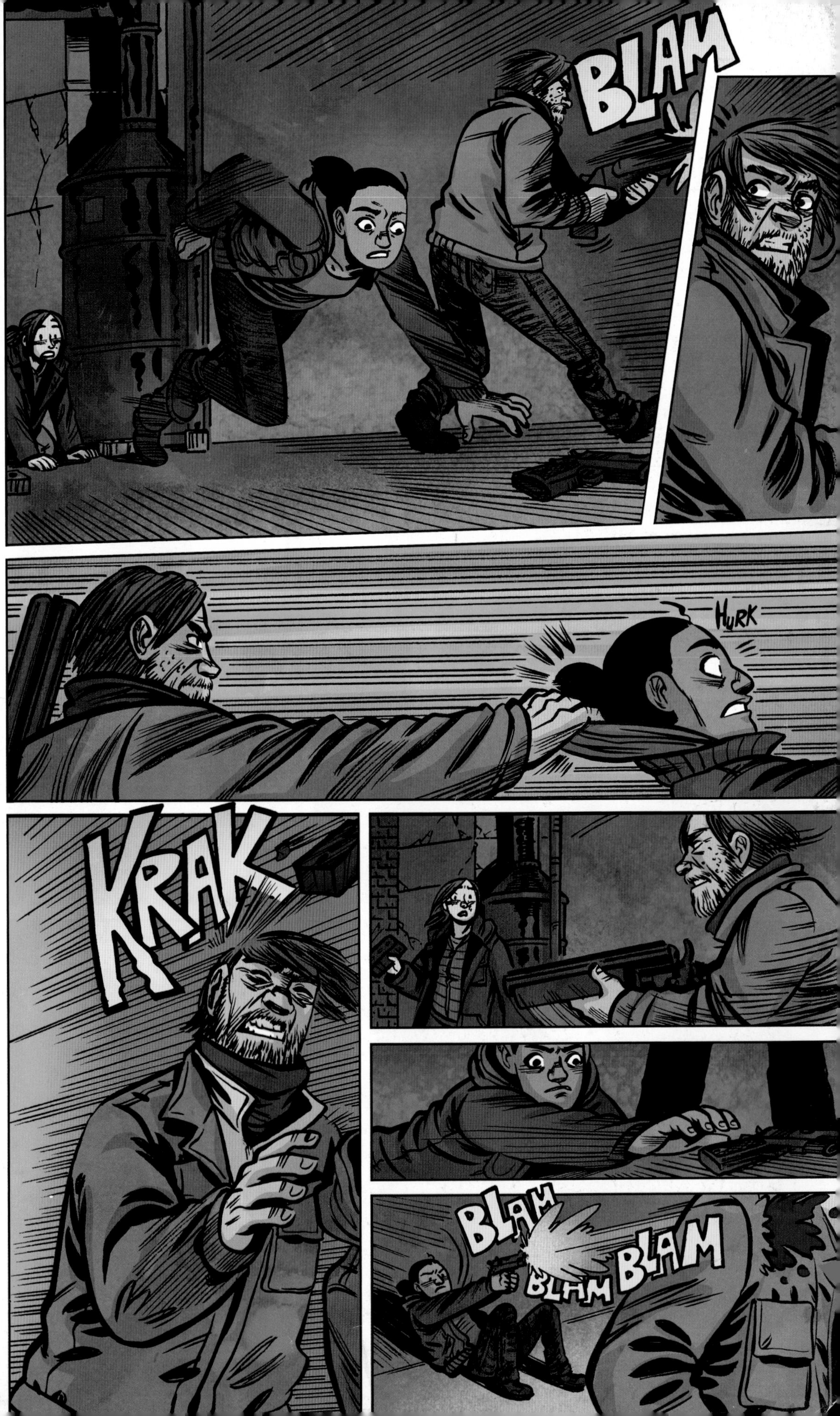
BLAM
HURK
KRAK
BLAM
BLAM
BLAM

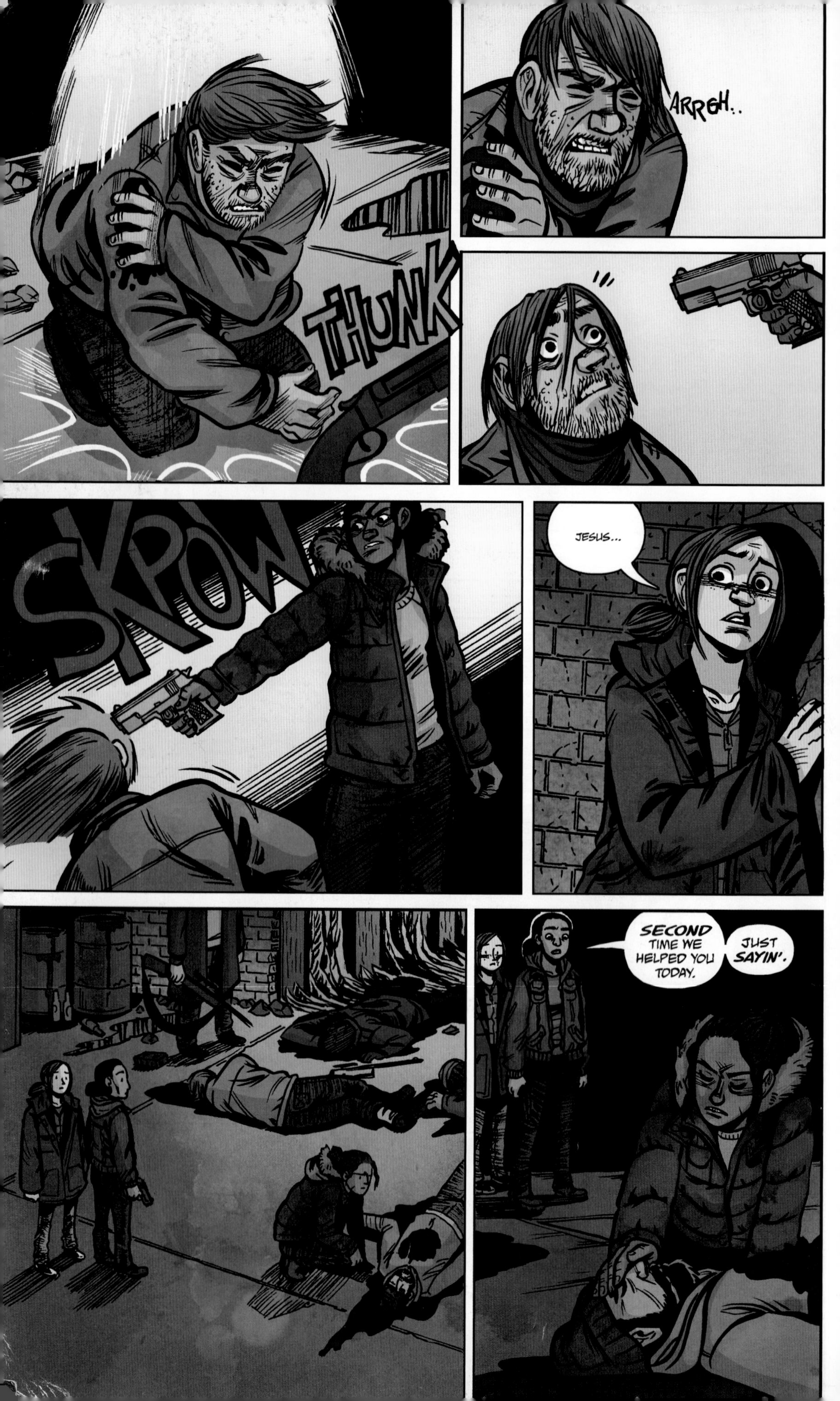

THUNK
ARRGH..
SKPOW
JESUS...
SECOND TIME WE HELPED YOU TODAY.
JUST SAYIN'.

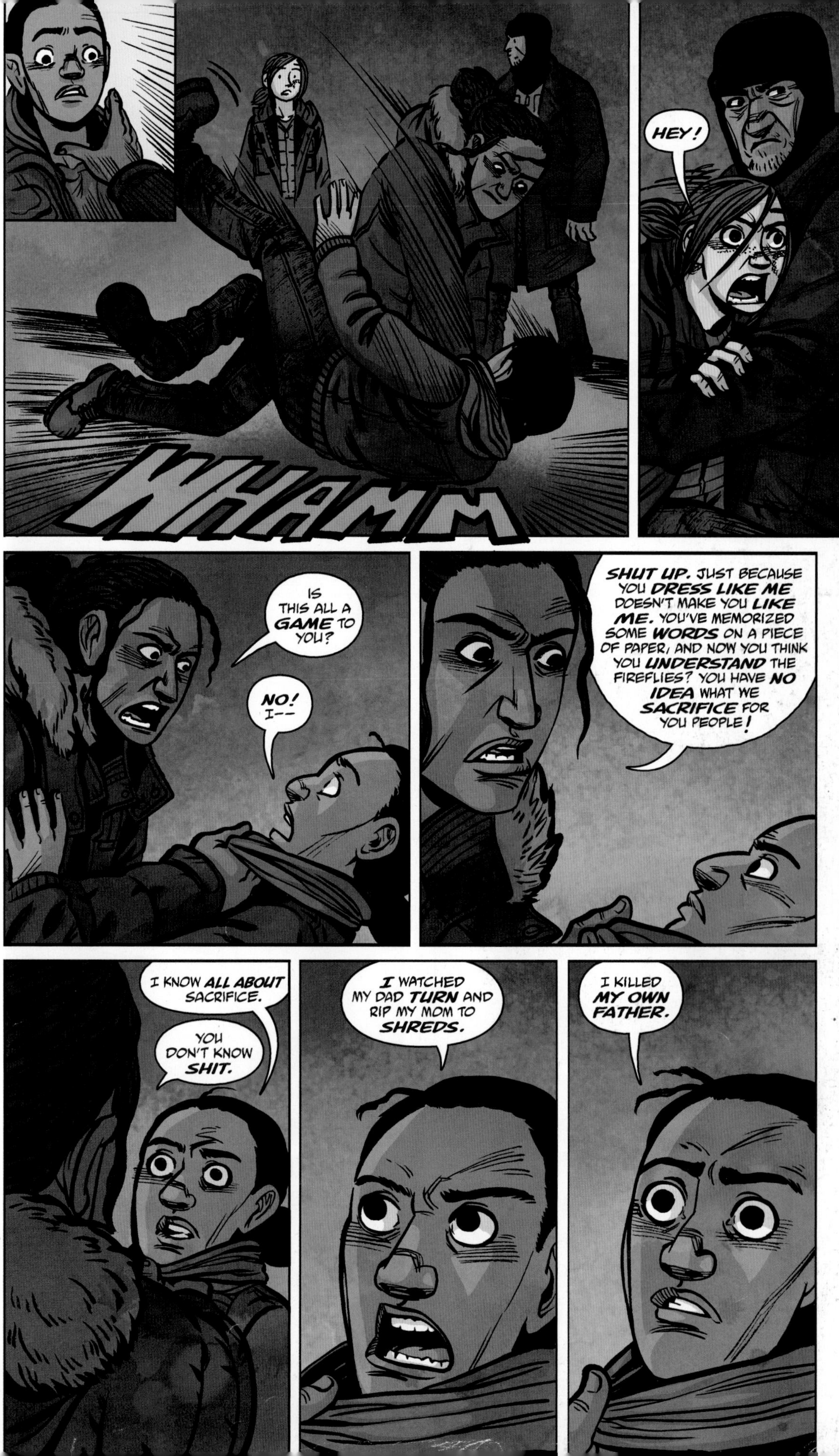
HEY!
WHAMM
IS THIS ALL A GAME TO YOU?
NO! I--
SHUT UP. JUST BECAUSE YOU DRESS LIKE ME DOESN'T MAKE YOU LIKE ME. YOU'VE MEMORIZED SOME WORDS ON A PIECE OF PAPER, AND NOW YOU THINK YOU UNDERSTAND THE FIREFLIES? YOU HAVE NO IDEA WHAT WE SACRIFICE FOR YOU PEOPLE!
I KNOW ALL ABOUT SACRIFICE.
YOU DON'T KNOW SHIT.
I WATCHED MY DAD TURN AND RIP MY MOM TO SHREDS.
I KILLED MY OWN FATHER.

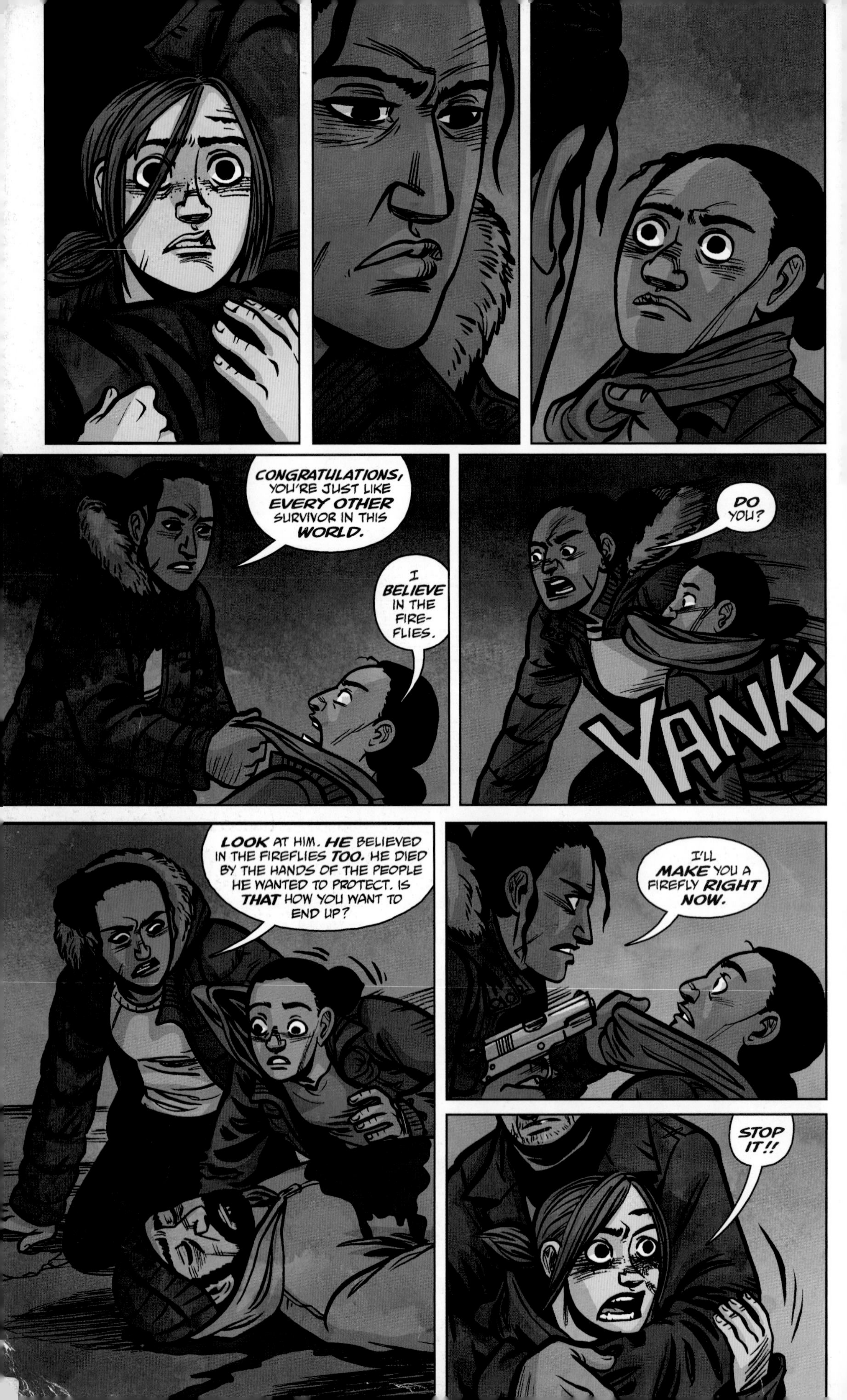
CONGRATULATIONS, YOU'RE JUST LIKE EVERY OTHER SURVIVOR IN THIS WORLD.
I BELIEVE IN THE FIRE-FLIES.
DO YOU?
YANK
LOOK AT HIM. HE BELIEVED IN THE FIREFLIES TOO. HE DIED BY THE HANDS OF THE PEOPLE HE WANTED TO PROTECT. IS THAT HOW YOU WANT TO END UP?
I'LL MAKE YOU A FIREFLY RIGHT NOW.
STOP IT!!

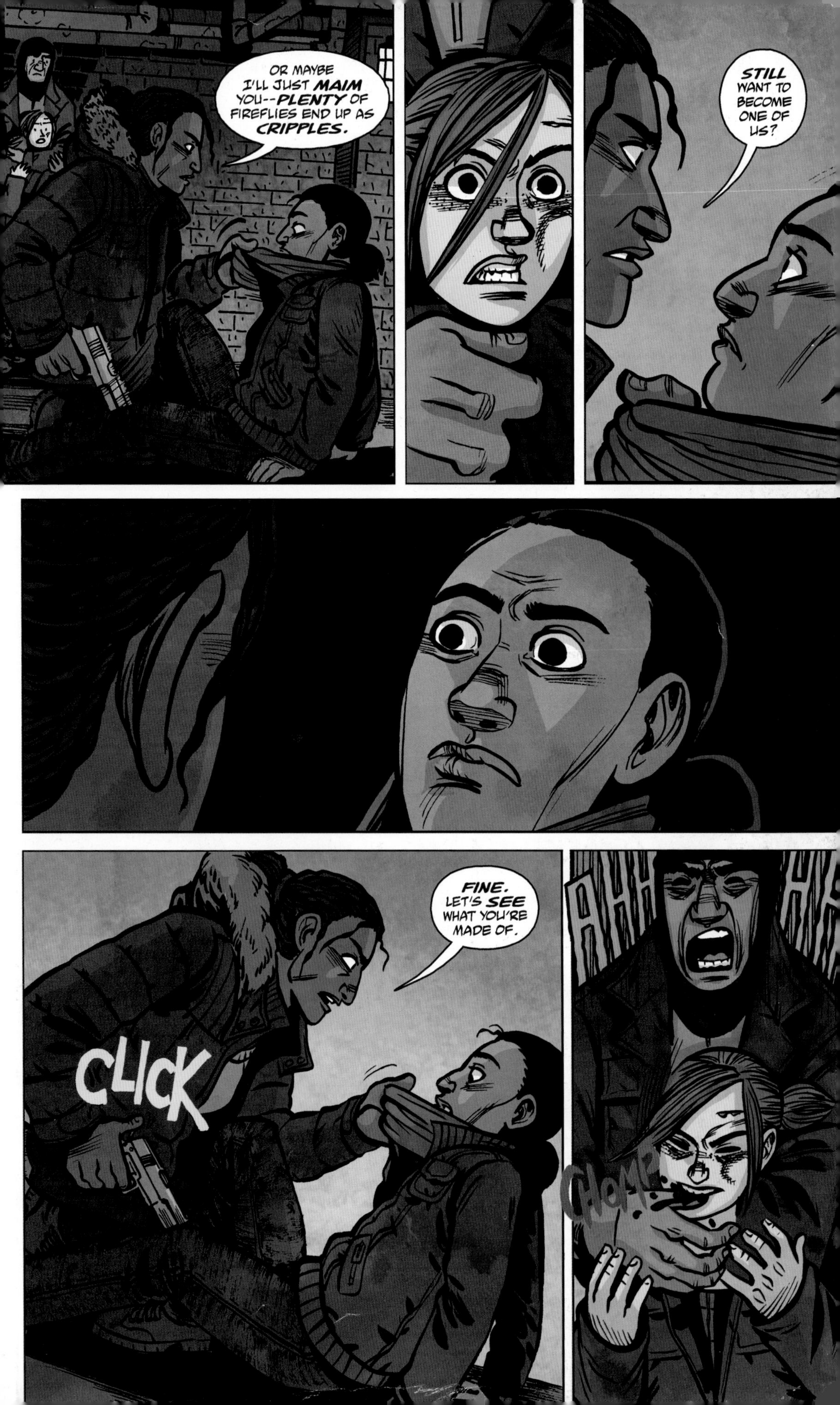

OR MAYBE I'LL JUST MAIM YOU--PLENTY OF FIREFLIES END UP AS CRIPPLES.
STILL WANT TO BECOME ONE OF US?
FINE. LET'S SEE WHAT YOU'RE MADE OF.
CLICK

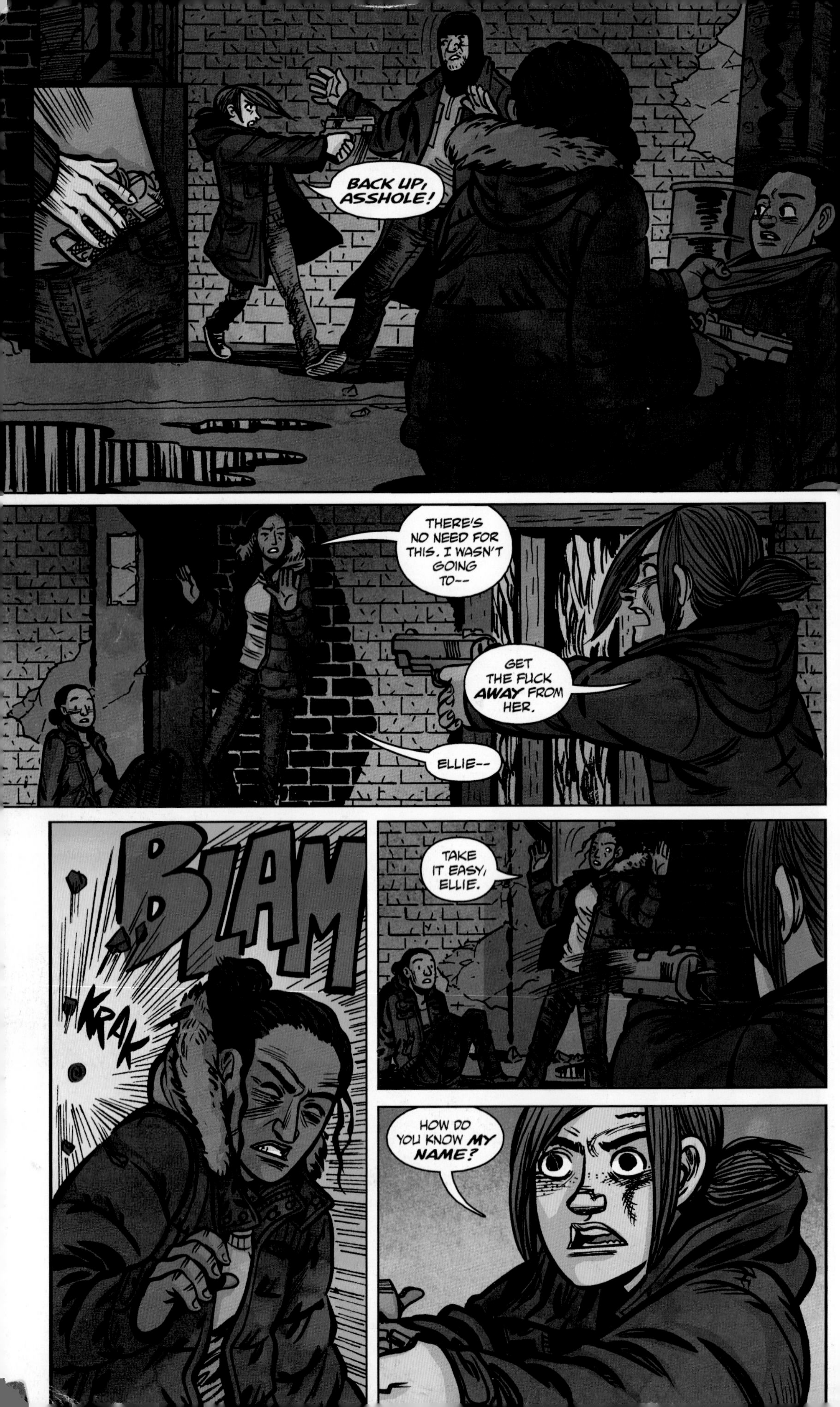
BACK UP, ASSHOLE!
THERE'S NO NEED FOR THIS. I WASN'T GOING TO--
GET THE FUCK AWAY FROM HER.
ELLIE--
BLAM
KRAK
TAKE IT EASY, ELLIE.
HOW DO YOU KNOW MY NAME?

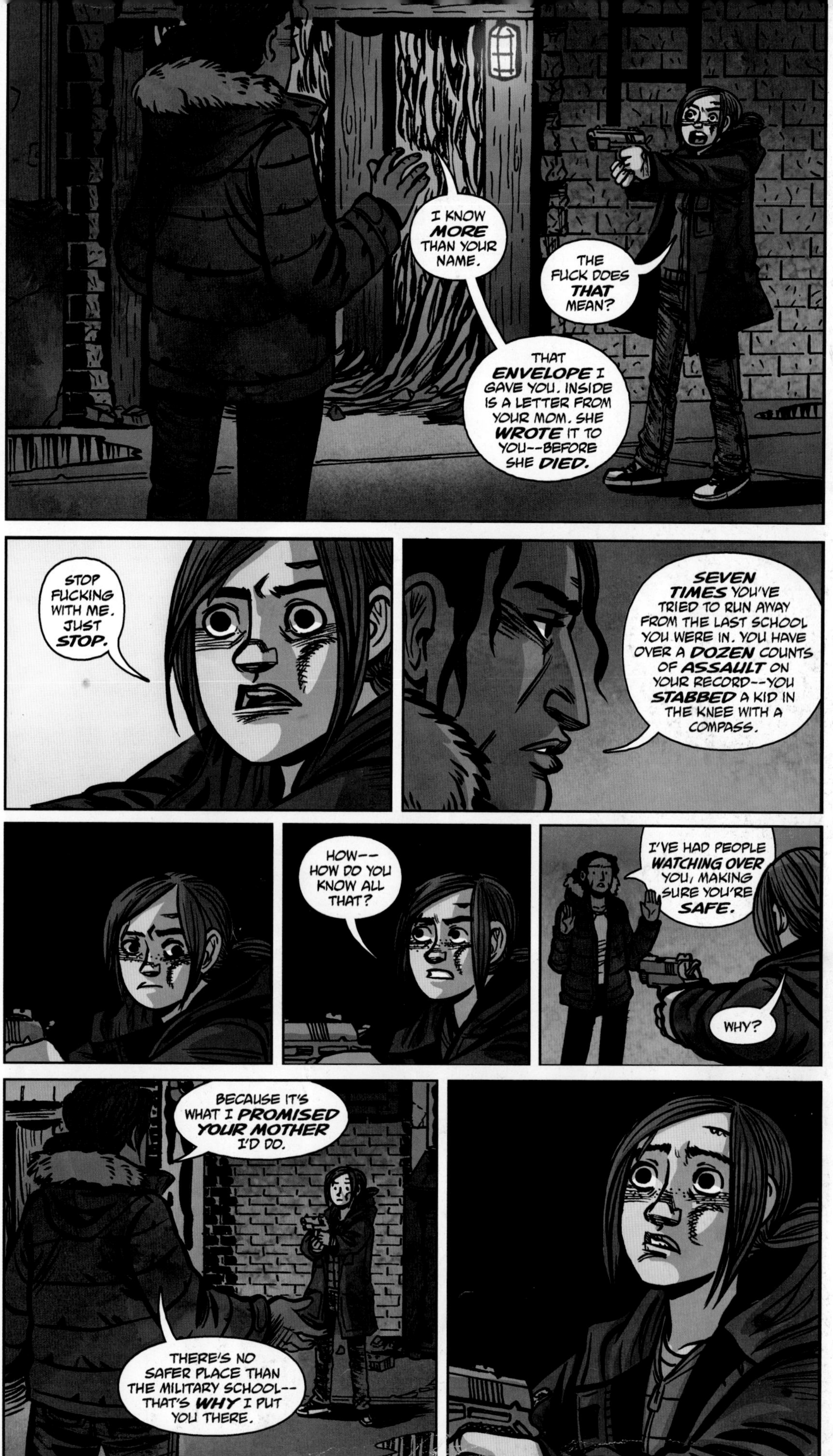
I KNOW MORE THAN YOUR NAME.
THE FUCK DOES THAT MEAN?
THAT ENVELOPE I GAVE YOU. INSIDE IS A LETTER FROM YOUR MOM. SHE WROTE IT TO YOU--BEFORE SHE DIED.
STOP FUCKING WITH ME. JUST STOP.
SEVEN TIMES YOU'VE TRIED TO RUN AWAY FROM THE LAST SCHOOL YOU WERE IN. YOU HAVE OVER A DOZEN COUNTS OF ASSAULT ON YOUR RECORD--YOU STABBED A KID IN THE KNEE WITH A COMPASS.
HOW-- HOW DO YOU KNOW ALL THAT?
I'VE HAD PEOPLE WATCHING OVER YOU, MAKING SURE YOU'RE SAFE.
WHY?
BECAUSE IT'S WHAT I PROMISED YOUR MOTHER I'D DO.
THERE'S NO SAFER PLACE THAN THE MILITARY SCHOOL-- THAT'S WHY I PUT YOU THERE.

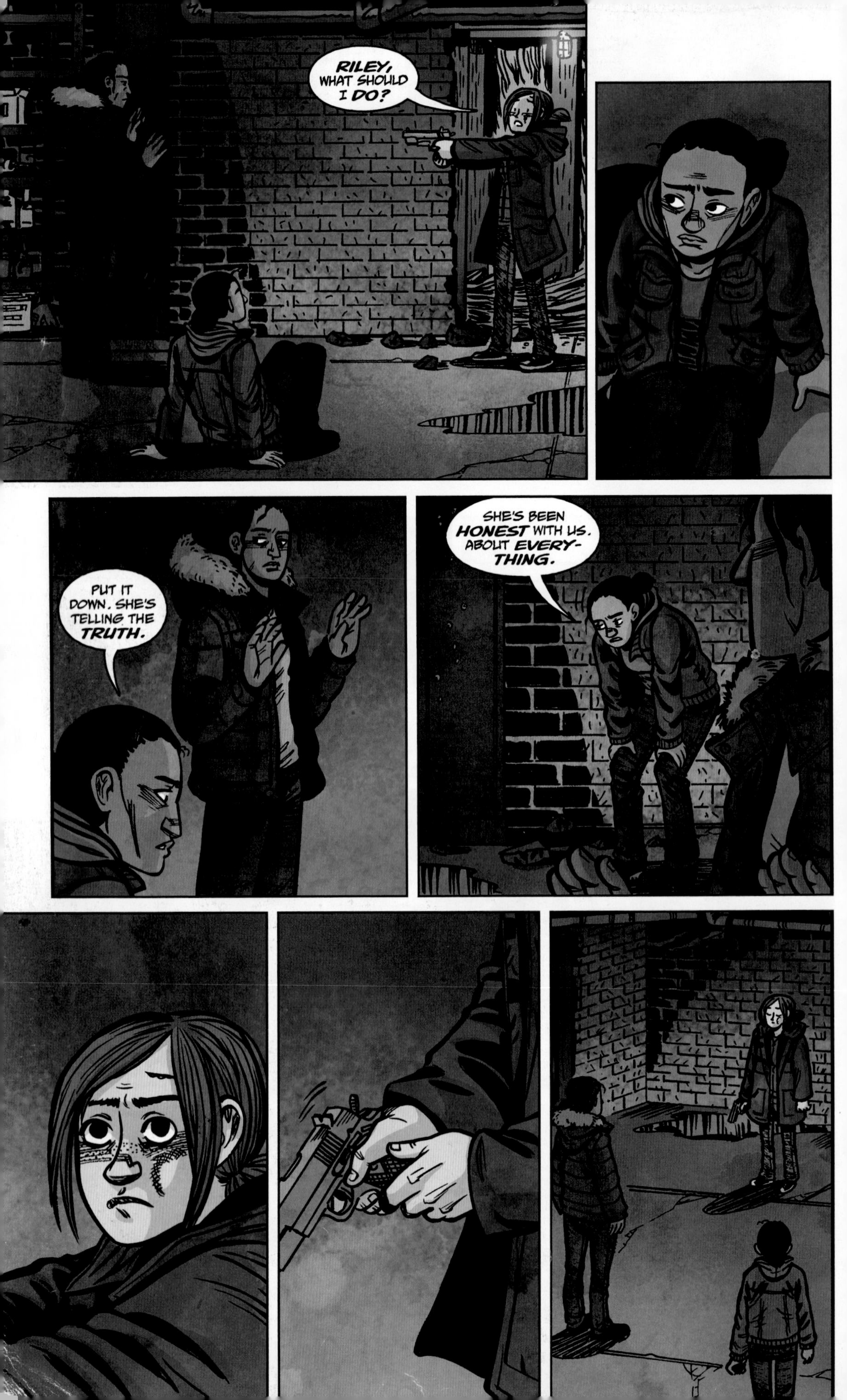
RILEY, WHAT SHOULD I DO?
PUT IT DOWN. SHE'S TELLING THE TRUTH.
SHE'S BEEN HONEST WITH US. ABOUT EVERY-THING.

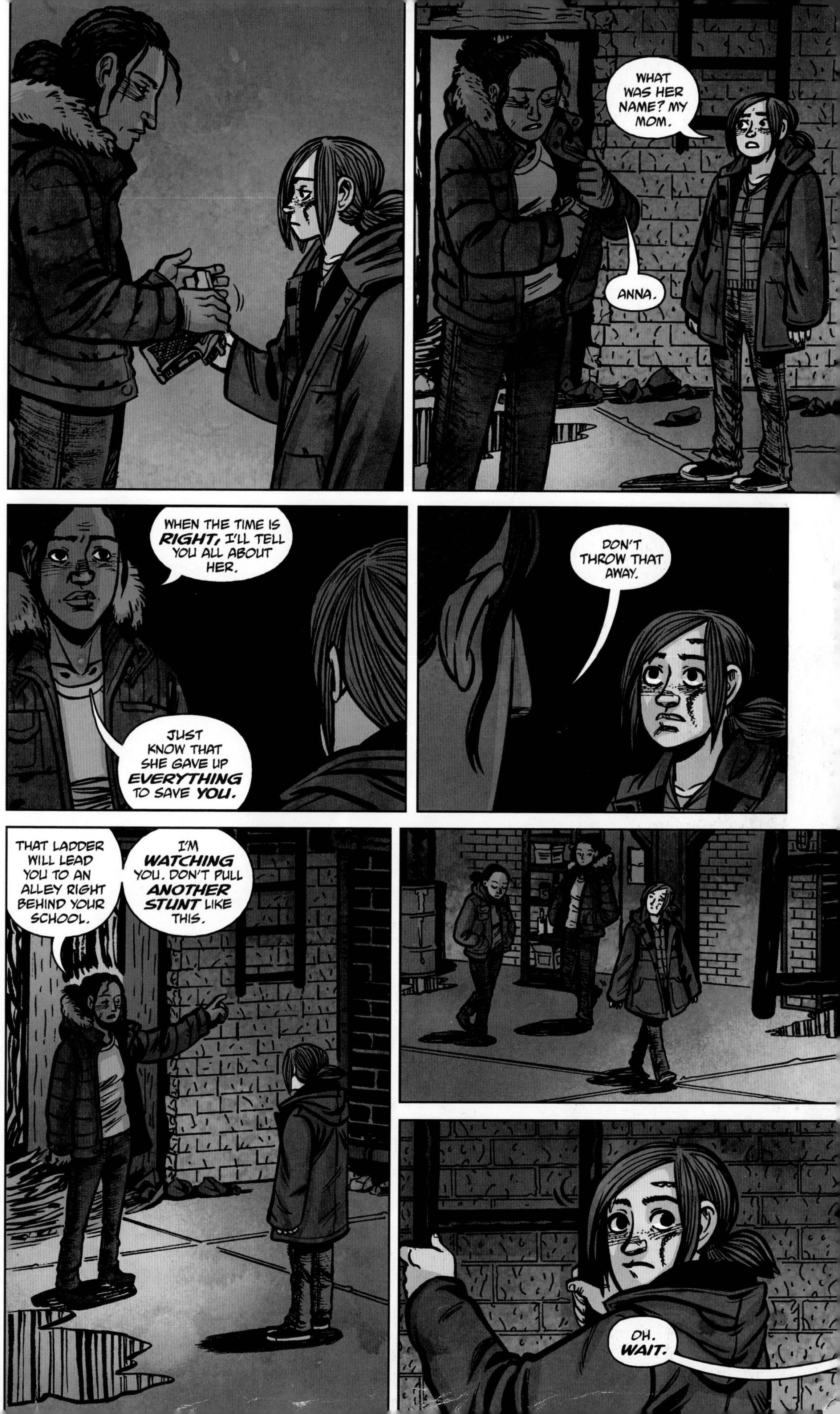
WHAT WAS HER NAME? MY MOM.
ANNA.
WHEN THE TIME IS RIGHT, I'LL TELL YOU ALL ABOUT HER.
JUST KNOW THAT SHE GAVE UP EVERYTHING TO SAVE YOU.
DON'T THROW THAT AWAY.
THAT LADDER WILL LEAD YOU TO AN ALLEY RIGHT BEHIND YOUR SCHOOL.
I'M WATCHING YOU. DON'T PULL ANOTHER STUNT LIKE THIS.
OH. WAIT.

IT WAS ANNA'S.

TRY NOT TO GET IT CONFISCATED.

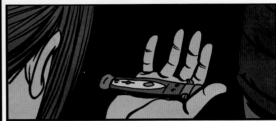

STOP

SAVE US

CREEKK

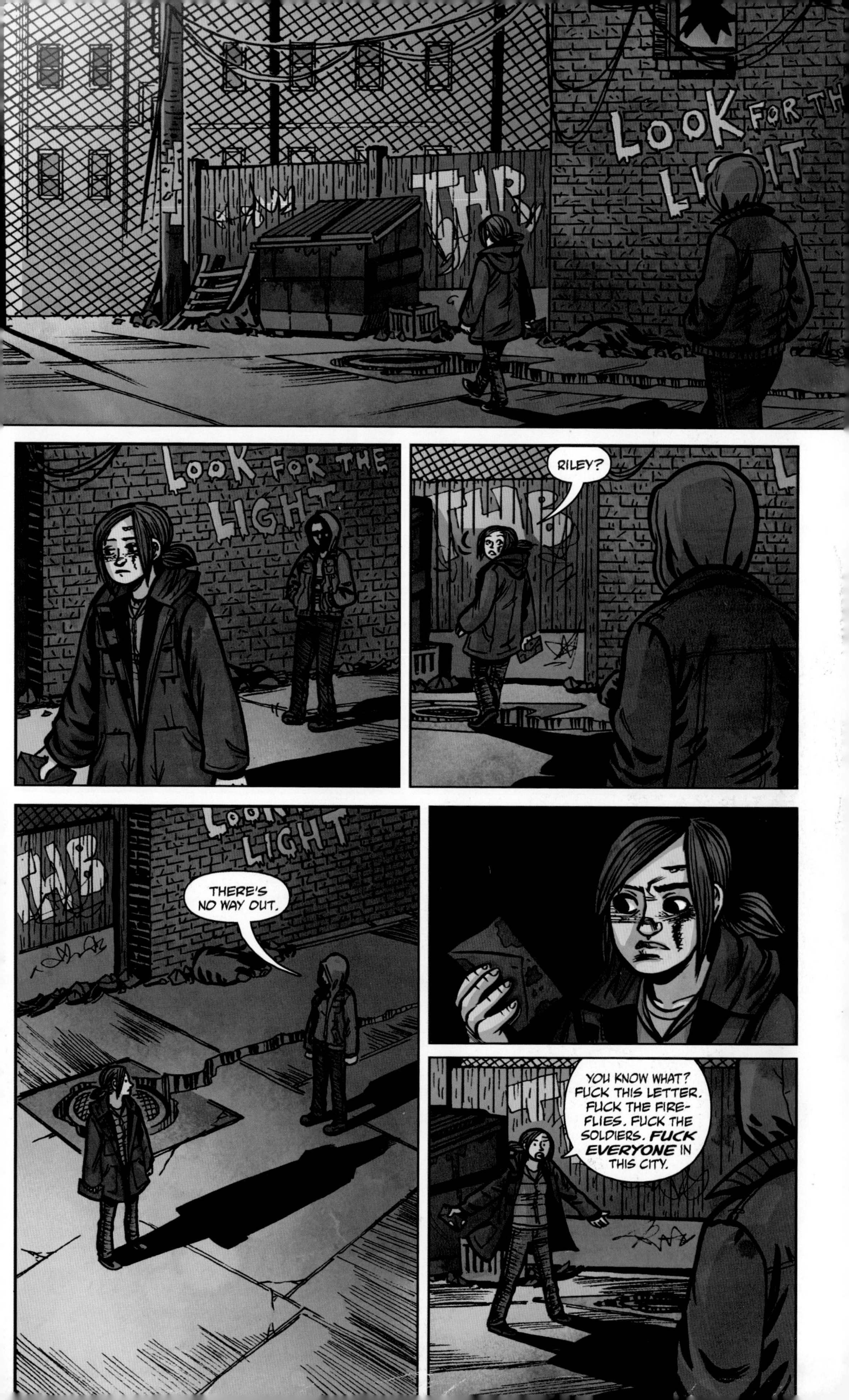
LOOK FOR THE LIGHT
THB
LOOK FOR THE LIGHT
RILEY?
THERE'S NO WAY OUT.
YOU KNOW WHAT? FUCK THIS LETTER. FUCK THE FIRE-FLIES. FUCK THE SOLDIERS. FUCK EVERYONE IN THIS CITY.

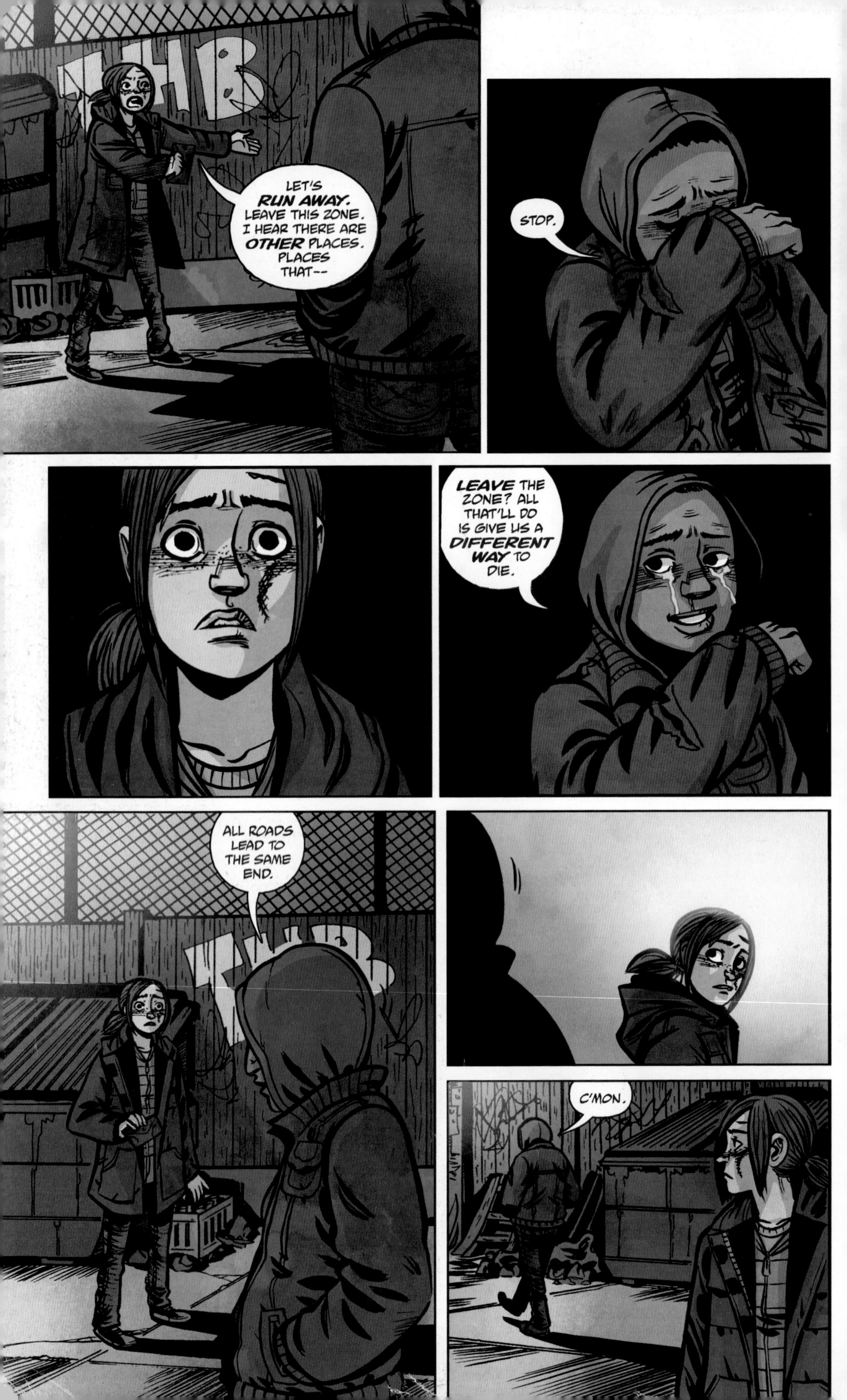
LET'S RUN AWAY. LEAVE THIS ZONE. I HEAR THERE ARE OTHER PLACES. PLACES THAT--
STOP.
LEAVE THE ZONE? ALL THAT'LL DO IS GIVE US A DIFFERENT WAY TO DIE.
ALL ROADS LEAD TO THE SAME END.
C'MON.

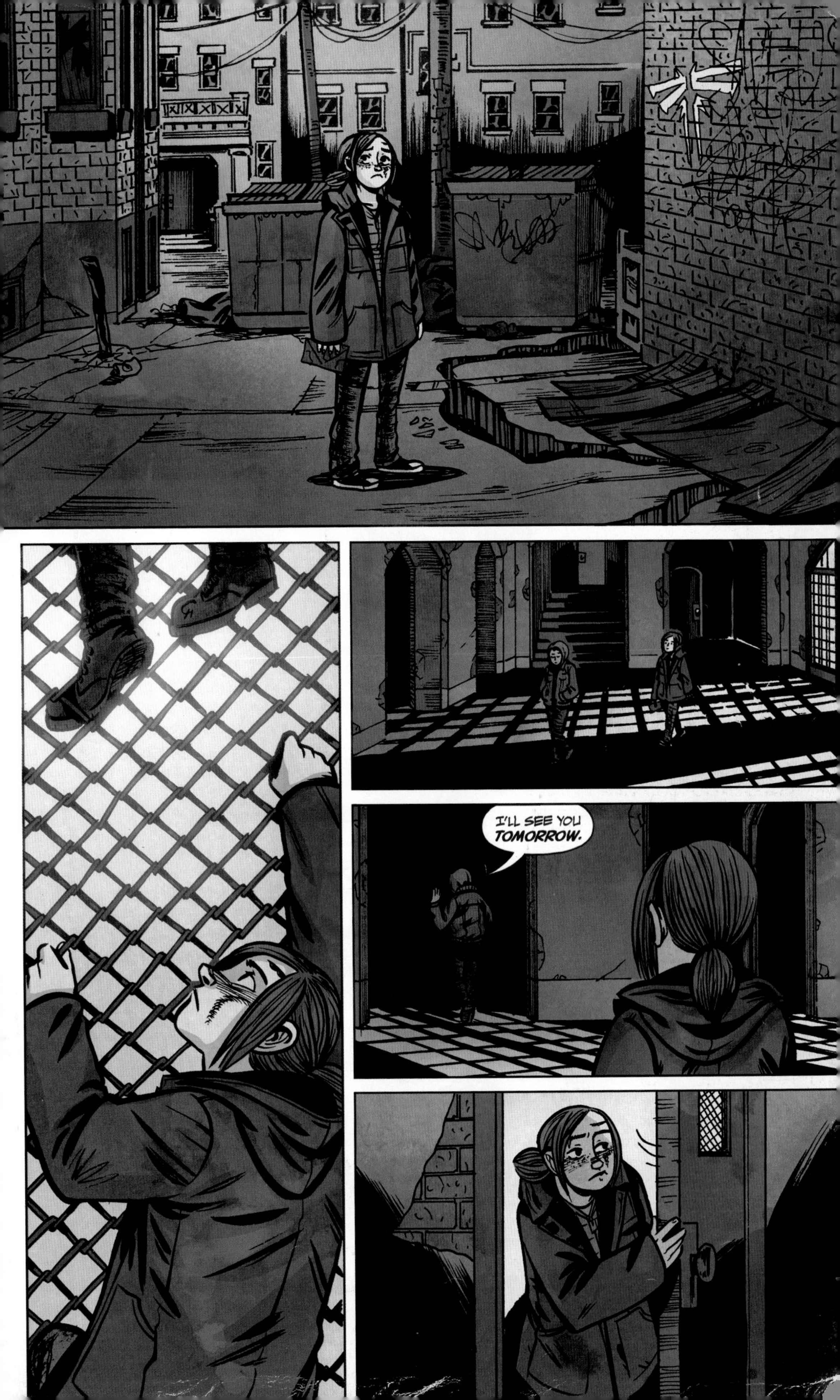
I'LL SEE YOU TOMORROW.

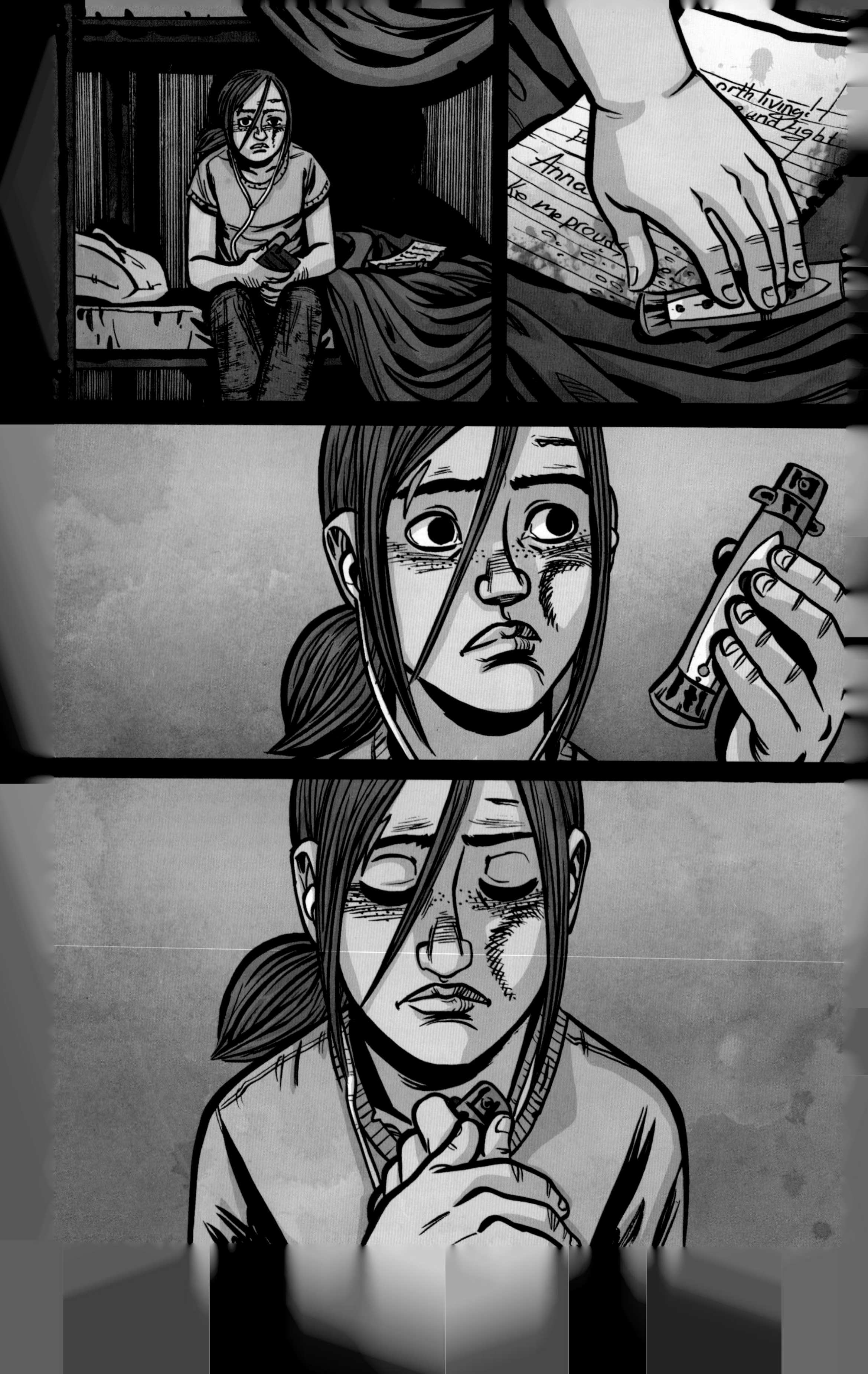
Anna

PREPARING FOR THE END

CONCEPT SKETCHES AND DESIGNS BY **FAITH ERIN HICKS**

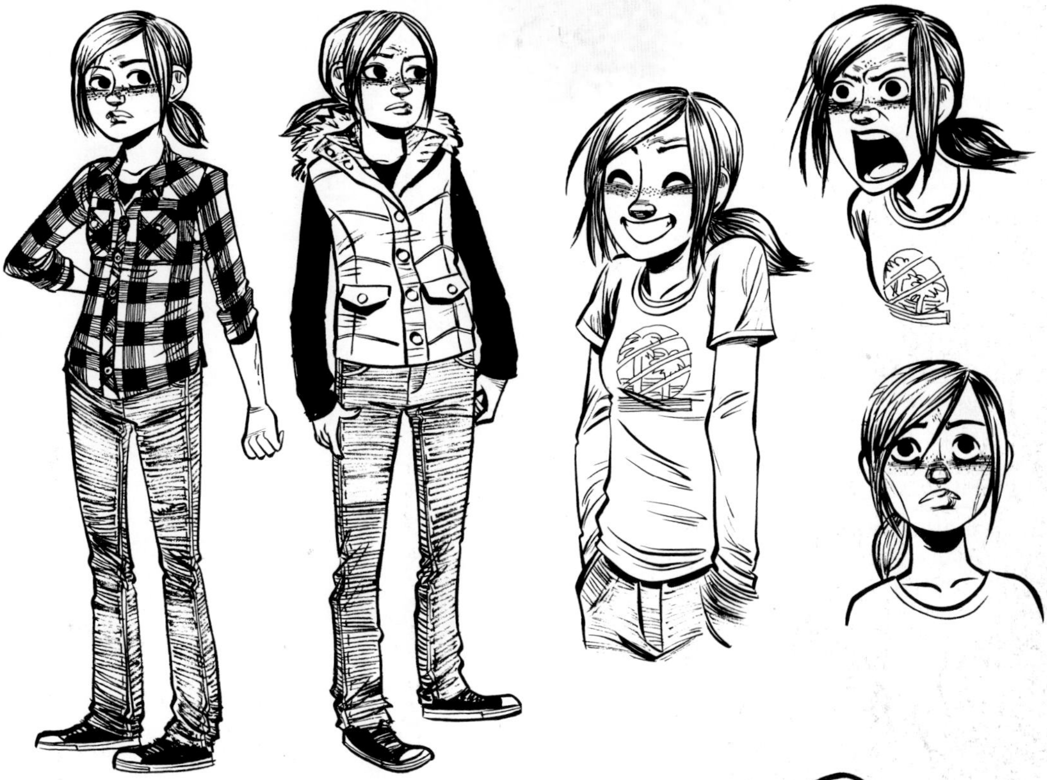

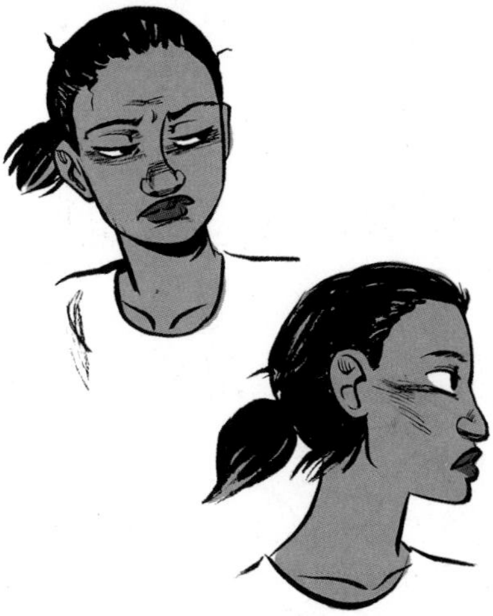

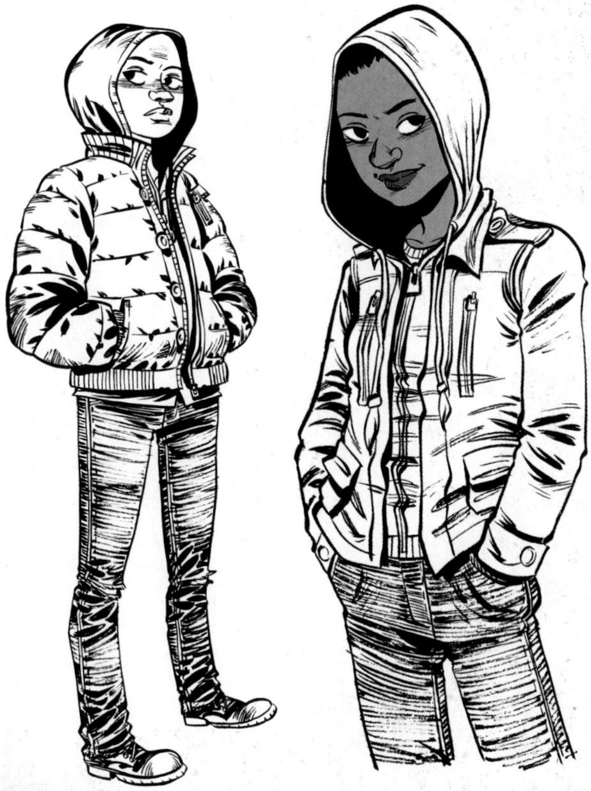

In translating Ellie and Riley to the page, Faith tried a variety of outfits and attitudes for each.

Right: Faith's Angel Knives design for the arcade cabinet of *The Turning* made its way into *The Last of Us* itself and was used for a T-shirt.

Below: More- and less-casual approaches to Marlene.

Opposite page, top: One of Faith's early concept sketches, made to get a feel for the post-Infection world.

Opposite page, bottom: Faith's initial ideas for the image used to promote *American Dreams* (the final version appears on page 2 of this collection).

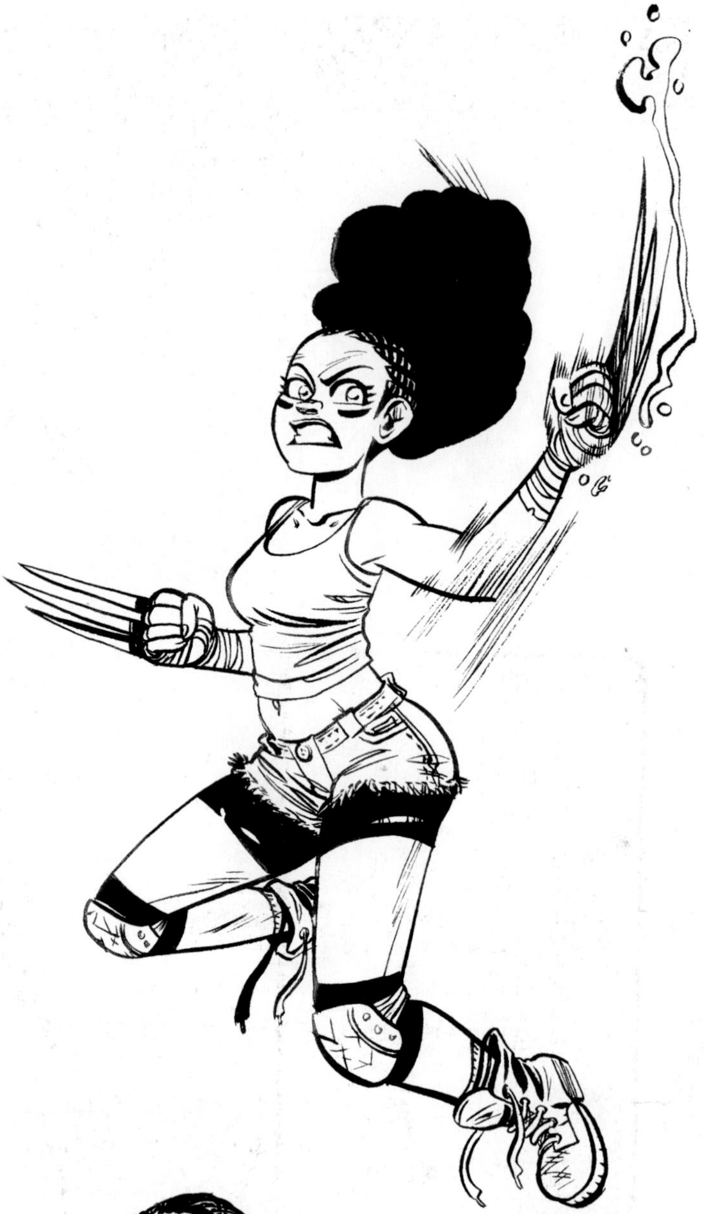

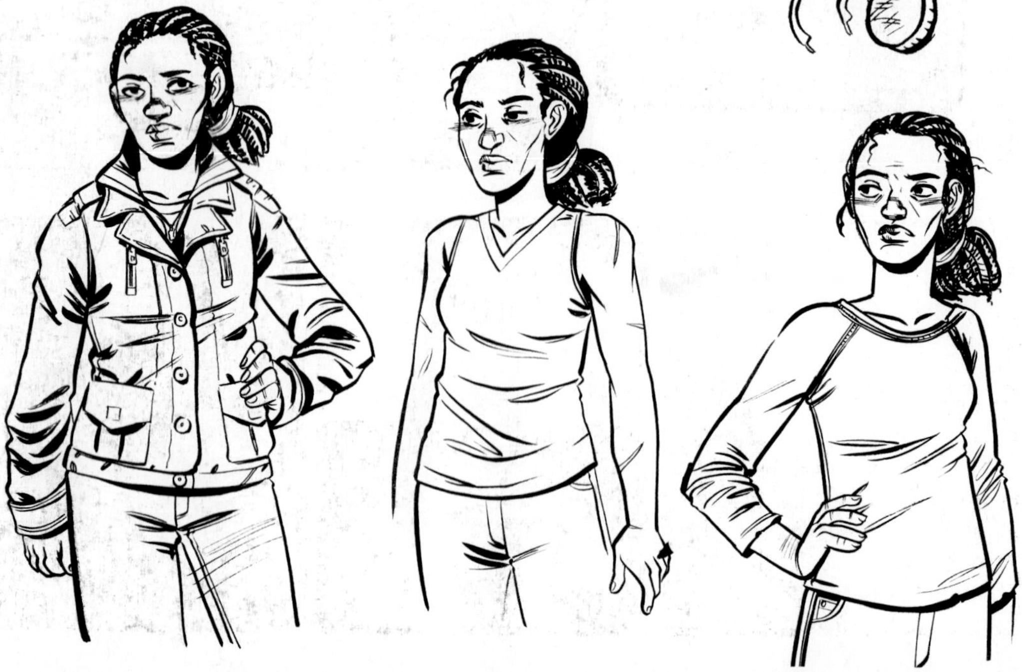

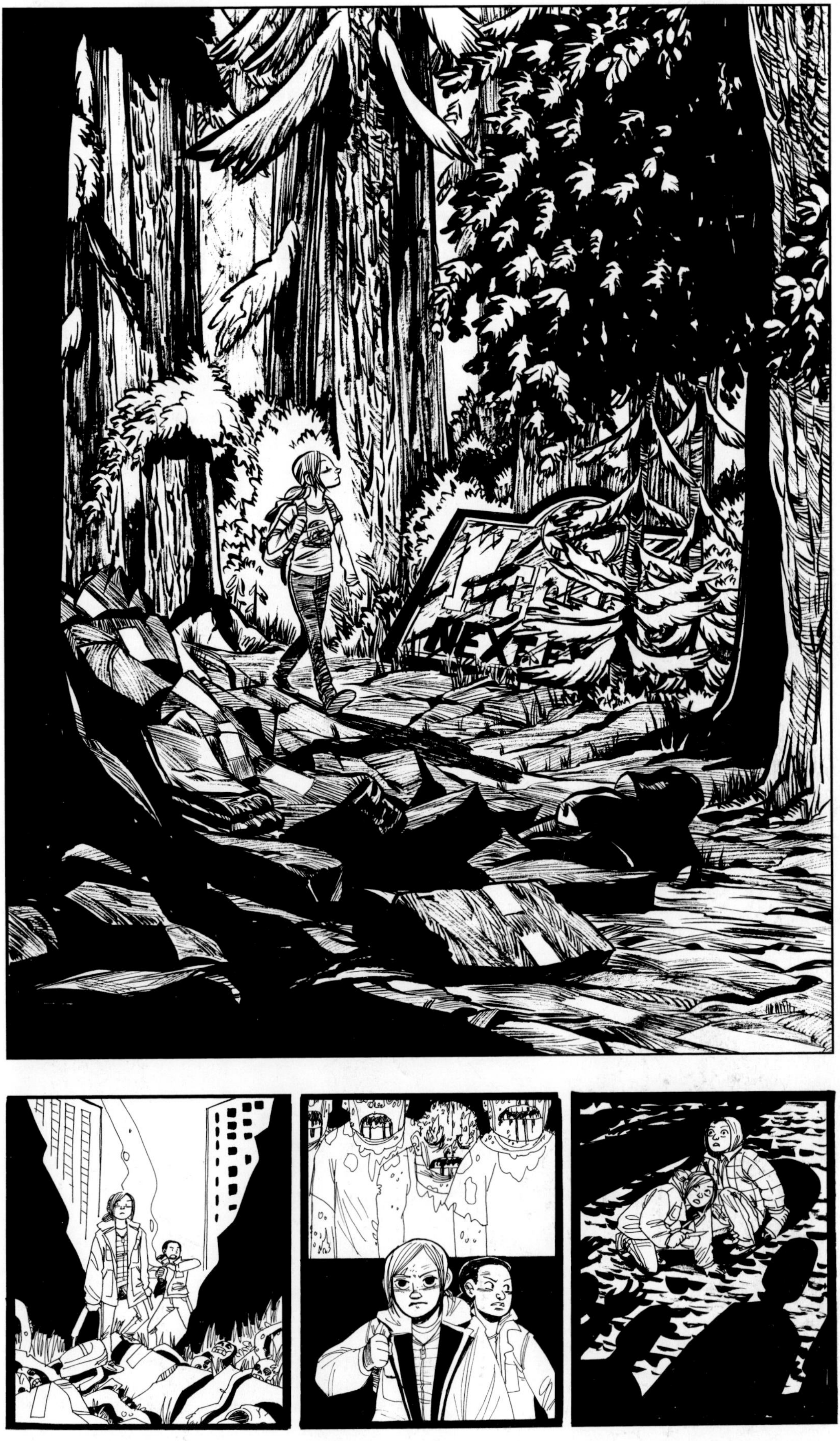
NEXT

JOURNEY INTO THE WORLD OF THE LAST OF US IN THE 176-PAGE ART BOOK!

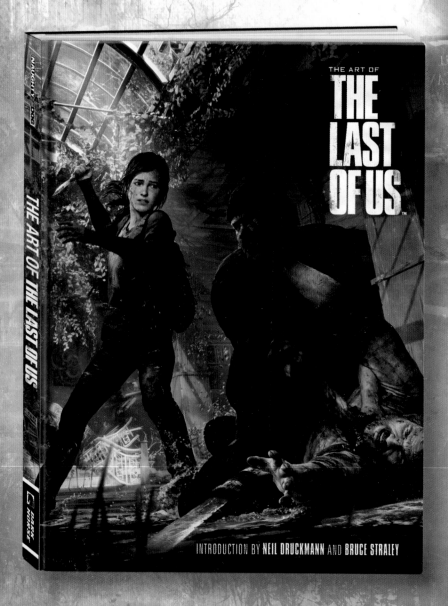

THE ART OF
THE
LAST
OF US™

INTRODUCTION BY **NEIL DRUCKMANN** AND **BRUCE STRALEY**